It's Not So Funny When It's *Your* Money

It's Not So Funny When It's *Your* Money

a lighthearted look at some typical financial behavior from a financial advisor's perspective

Stuart Horowitz, MBA, RFC, CFP® with
Andrew G. Rosenberg, CFP®, Esq.
and Ellen Rosenthal

iUniverse, Inc.
New York Lincoln Shanghai

It's Not So Funny When It's Your Money
a lighthearted look at some typical financial behavior from a financial
advisor's perspective

iUniverse books may be ordered through booksellers or by contacting:

iUniverse
2021 Pine Lake Road, Suite 100
Lincoln, NE 68512
www.iuniverse.com
1-800-Authors (1-800-288-4677)

Andrew Stuart Asset Management, 12510 W. Atlantic Blvd. Coral Springs, Florida
33071. (954) 510-1100. info@andrewstuart.net www.andrewstuart.net

FIRST EDITION

ISBN-13: 978-0-595-40916-7 (pbk)
ISBN-13: 978-0-595-67850-1 (cloth)
ISBN-13: 978-0-595-85279-6 (ebk)
ISBN-10: 0-595-40916-4 (pbk)
ISBN-10: 0-595-67850-5 (cloth)
ISBN-10: 0-595-85279-3 (ebk)

Printed in the United States of America

for Ilene

CONTENTS

ACKNOWLEDGEMENTS

First off, I must express my love and admiration for my wife, Ilene. She has always been so supportive, patient, and inspirational. My son and best buddy Matthew's passion for life is awesome. My daughter, Stephanie, puts a smile on my face daily and can light up a room in an instant. Not a day goes by that I don't recognize how lucky I am to have such amazing people in my life.

Andy patiently waited for this book to be completed and shouldered much of the burden of running our practice during the crunch times. Thanks for being the greatest partner anyone can hope for. Get some sleep, will ya?

The supporting cast at Andrew Stuart Asset Management Group makes my job so much easier and takes such good care of all of our clients. Remember to strive for perfection (ok—*nearly flawless execution*).

Ellen, you made this book a reality. When I started to falter and procrastinate, you were there to push me along and keep me on track. The personal experiences and anecdotes you contributed most definitely brought this project to completion.

People come into your life at different points and time and you may not realize at that moment the influence they may have on you. Looking back now, it all makes sense. Amanda, wherever *you* are, thanks for helping get this off the ground. I hope this book finds you and puts a smile on your face. Kristie, wherever *you* are, your contributions are appreciated.

Jesse, your great aunt Esther, one of my favorite clients, led me to you. It's about being in the right place at the right time. You were the last piece of the puzzle that took almost three years to complete.

Thank you to all of our clients. I have learned as much from you as I hope you have learned from me.

INTRODUCTION

"Everything in moderation." These are the words I live by and convey to all those who seek my advice as a friend and financial consultant.

Balance is one of those achievements that can only really be measured by the person attempting to achieve it—whether it is 70% work and 30% play, 90% love and 10% money, or 50% peanut butter and 50% jelly. While finding that balance may be a lifelong journey, it can be a pleasurable one.

This is my attempt at guiding you along that journey.

All of the characters in this book are fictitious, but they are fictions drawn from personal experience. Over the years, I've met with more than 2,300 prospects and clients, each with their own personal stories, struggles, and successes. What follows are my reflections, based on these real-life encounters, designed to address the intellectual concepts that so many authors have attempted to explain. With their creative characters, comedic quotes, and thoughtful solutions, these narratives will, I hope, keep you entertained while helping you embrace the valuable lessons they hold. And I hope they will prompt you to look in the mirror. Can you see yourself in any (or many) of these stories?

Regardless of your financial knowledge, you'll inevitably face some sort of life-altering monetary decision every five to ten years. It's almost like a fairy tale....

Once upon a time, in two tiny villages, there lived a bright-eyed young man named Peter and a lively young woman named Sue. They each had heard of a far-off place called "College," and when they applied to go there, they each qualified for financial aid. With tears in their eyes, they left their parents' gingerbread cottages to face the difficult challenges set for them by elderly creatures called Professors. They passed every test, and when it was over, each went out into the world to slay a dragon (or find a job, as we would call it). This they both succeeded in doing, and were rewarded with 401(k) options and benefit packages. One warm spring morning, Sue bumped into Peter, who was filling his cup with cool water at the...um, Water Cooler. They were both instantly bewitched. They mar-

ried, opened their first joint checking account, and filed their first joint income tax return. Although they thought they were "just looking" that day the realtor showed them the brand-new three-bedroom gingerbread bungalow, they made a deposit on their first home and applied for a mortgage.

Along came babies one and two, as well as the expenses and wonders of raising children (not to mention life insurance decisions). Years went by, the children grew, and the couple began to consider education savings plans. They also knew they would like to retire someday—no one slays dragons forever. Sooner than it seemed possible, the children left home tearfully to try their own luck in that far-off land of College. The kids soon found their own enchantments—some of which Peter and Sue approved, some of which they did not. Time passed. Their children had children. Peter and Sue began to look around them at what they had accumulated, and knew they needed to decide what to leave as a legacy, and how to leave it. They wanted their children to know their wishes—neither of them wanted to be put into a nursing home unless there was no other choice. On summer evenings, when the family was in town, they all sat on their gingerbread porch and watched the sun set. "Don't ever pull the plug on me," Sue told the family on these occasions. "Some wizard will find a miracle cure." Peter said that when his time came, he wanted them to let him go without a fuss.

Okay, maybe the Brothers Grimm don't have anything to worry about just yet, but the point is that there are a lot of financial decisions that many of us will have to make under similar circumstances as we go through life. While sifting through this collection of stories you'll soon discover the majority of these decisions carry some overlapping questions and themes:

- All too often financial decisions are based purely on emotions. Beware. Financial decisions based on feelings are short-term fixes with long-term consequences. As a financial adviser, I do not manage my own portfolio. What I can do for others, I cannot do for myself.

- Doing nothing is a conscious decision. If you avoid controlling your finances or taking action, you may miss valuable opportunities or face avoidable consequences.

- When does money lead to greater happiness, and when does it blind us to the happiness we have?

- Who are the fictitious Joneses we so often compare ourselves to? Is this a realistic comparison?

There are no definitive, one-size-fits-all solutions to any of these familiar questions and dilemmas, but hopefully as you read through these brief stories you'll unearth your own. If nothing else, once you've read this book I'd like for you to take a step back when facing your financial objectives and search for a more logical approach.

When reading this, I ask that you keep an open mind, relate to the situations that you yourself have faced, laugh a little (or a lot), and take note of the professional perspectives provided to help you deal with each situation.

I would consider my efforts a success if one day several years from now you remember how foolish "Fishing Rod" or "Jackpot Judy" seemed when they faced the situation you might be facing that day.

Remember, it's not so funny when it's *your* money.

LIFE PLANNING

"Money can't buy happiness. You also need high-yield
stocks, prime real estate, and a solid credit rating!"

Do I Need Financial Or Marriage Counseling?

"My wife Mary and I have been married for forty-seven years and not once have we had an argument serious enough to consider divorce; murder, yes, but divorce, never."

-Jack Benny-

In their early fifties, John and Sara appear to have the ideal marriage. John has a wonderful sense of humor and Sara expertly sets up the punch lines. Neither looks a day over 45, and John can be seen beaming with pride as they walk hand in hand together. From the outside looking in, they are the couple you want to emulate.

But things aren't as rosy as they might appear. Money is something they rarely agree on. John believes that the only way to invest is to go for it all. He consistently looks for the "hot" stock. Sometimes John's investments pay off big, but most of the time he walks away with pennies on the dollar. Sara, on the other hand, is ultra-conservative. She prefers very low-risk vehicles, willingly foregoing any big paydays.

Retirement is also a major point of contention in their marriage. John and Sara have always been on different pages when it comes to planning for their retirement years. John would like to retire at age 55. John's dad, Bob, had the opportunity to retire at 55 but decided to wait another five years. He had big plans for his retirement years with John's mom and wanted to make sure they had more than enough money to enjoy them. He could almost taste the bass he was going to catch during their fishing trips. He shivered at the thought of tooling around in the garage with his '68 Corvette. A history buff, he'd planned three trips to famous World War II battle sites in Europe. Exactly fourteen months to the day prior to retirement, Bob had a major heart attack and died suddenly. John's dad was 50 pounds overweight, loved his bacon in the morning, and hadn't seen a doctor in fifteen years. John never shared the details of his dad's dreams with Sara.

Sara comes from a family of savers. While her dad earned a great living running his own electrical business, the family never indulged itself. There were no extravagant vacations. They bought Buicks when they could easily have afforded Cadillacs. They shopped at Kmart when they could have browsed the racks at Bloomingdale's. Sara's parents always had cash on hand and rebuffed all credit card offers. Their habits were shaped by the belief that financial catastrophe lurked behind every corner, ready to ruin them if they let their guard down for a moment. Sara never shared with John the details of her family's attitude towards money.

Drawing from her own experiences, Sara fears they will run out of money at some point during retirement. She feels they should keep working at least until 62 to add to their retirement nest egg.

Over the last several years they've been dealing with their differences in an all too common way—by not discussing them. Now, with retirement slowly creeping up, it has become increasingly difficult to avoid the topic. As a result of their fighting, Sara has gone to bed in tears more times in the past year than in the prior thirty years of their marriage.

Professional Perspective

Money is said to be the greatest cause of arguments in a marriage. It often leads to a need for some type of counseling. In fact, I've found that in order to do my job as a financial consultant, I've often had to provide a form of what amounts to marriage counseling.

When Sara and John came to meet with me for the first time, there was clearly tension in the air. I began the meeting the way I typically do by asking them why they were here and what they were hoping to accomplish at our meeting. John spoke first. He was especially guarded. His comments were factual as he detailed the value of their accounts and the current level of annual savings they achieved. Sara sat quietly, but her face was a picture of distress, impatience, and frustration.

After fifteen minutes, I interjected—the direction of this meeting was never going to get us to the Promised Land. "John," I asked, "if money were not a factor, what would your life look like tomorrow?" While John squirmed in his chair, Sara began to perk up with an interested look on her face. John asked me to repeat the question. "How would your life change if you suddenly had $5 million deposited in your bank account? Would you live your life any differently than you do now?" Sara's elbows were no longer on the table supporting her head. John thought long and hard. He couldn't think of one thing that he would change about his life. He had a fulfilling career as a graphic artist for a major film company. His work was challenging and we already knew how much he loved his wife. I asked him "Why is it so important to retire at 55 if your life is so fulfilling?" With tears in the corners of his eyes, he began to talk about his dad's death and the way it had made him feel all these years. Sara began to cry too. She said, "John, why haven't you ever told me any of this?" John never realized the impact his dad's passing had on his approach to life.

From there, the meeting went a completely different direction. Both John and Sara spoke openly about their concerns over money—John not wanting to miss out on the opportunity to enjoy the money and Sara not wanting to lose the money. John was also a picture of health; he had a much lower risk of heart trouble than his father. Amid the emotional outbreaks, we were able to discuss their finances. Our preliminary analysis indicated that John and Sara could, with a high degree of confidence, retire when John turned 55. They would not outlive their money, and a high degree of risk was unnecessary to achieve their goals.

Sara couldn't contain herself. It was as if a weight had been removed from her shoulders. She began to speak of how she'd always wanted a little place on Florida's west coast for weekend getaways. John, on the other hand, pulled a 180° and said that he really enjoyed working. He couldn't see himself calling it quits at 55.

Oh, brother!

It's a Balancing Act

"What's the use of happiness? It can't buy you money."

-Henny Youngman-

Man's Best Friend

Dr. David Larson was a very successful dermatologist. His patients and his practice always came first. While dermatology was not the most exciting of specialties, there were few midnight emergencies. Acne may be problematic but it's rarely, if ever, a matter of life and death. He maintained two offices and a ten-person staff. He never had the desire to bring on a partner—no one could provide the bedside manner that he could, and he was unwilling to jeopardize his flawless reputation in order to make a few extra bucks. He preferred to remain solely responsible for the fate of his career. With his professional success, however, came sacrifices in his personal life.

Almost twenty-six years after graduating from medical school and starting his practice, this 56-year-old good-looking divorcé with two alienated teenage kids and a bitter ex-wife was ready to retire. He found himself facing a new life for which he was not prepared.

With his newfound freedom, David felt it was time to put his priorities in order. He initially sought to rekindle his relationship with his ex-wife and children, but unfortunately it was too late—the damage had been done. His ex-wife was now fifty pounds lighter and dating someone new. His children were at the age where "spending time with dad" ran a close second to water torture on their list of activities to be avoided.

He then tried hanging out with his old buddies Cliff and Norm, also divorced, but they spent so much of their free time at the local bar, talking about nothing, that their favorite bar stools had taken on the shapes of their posteriors. This quickly lost its appeal for David. Thus, he was left by his lonesome, indulging in steak and beer while watching Western re-runs. It wasn't long before David became tired of being his own best friend and decided maybe it was time to re-enter the dating world.

Despite his good looks, David could never get past the first date; his lack of social skills haunted him, and his pickiness didn't make things any easier. Over the next six months he tried Internet dating services, personal ads, and blind dates, but nothing worked. So David did what any desperate rich bachelor would do. He tried to woo the women with his money. Rather than showering the ladies with gifts, however, he showered himself in the hopes of impressing them. He bought himself a condo on the ocean, a platinum Rolex, a sporty new Mercedes, and a 30-foot sailboat, even though he hadn't found the time for sailing lessons. He bought every virile luxury he could find, but with that kind of bait in South Florida, he found he didn't like the women he was able to catch. He was better dressed now, but David was back to square one.

Hoping to conquer his loneliness, he bought a Hungarian Vischla puppy and named him Bow Tox (how fitting). David was ecstatic that he finally had a companion, someone (or at least some*thing*) to love him. Bow Tox greatly enjoyed going for walks and was a big hit at the dog park.

It happened by chance one Sunday afternoon. Bow Tox was especially frisky and took off the very moment David unleashed him. David franticly tried to keep pace but Bow Tox was already fifty yards ahead. David began to panic at the thought of losing his pal. Almost as quickly as Bow Tox had taken off, the dog stopped suddenly next to a cute purebred poodle. The owner of the poodle, Nancy, was an attractive middle-aged woman who had recently retired from her successful law practice. David had seen her around the park before, and had even noticed that she never wore any rings on the fourth finger of her left hand. They smiled at each other, introduced themselves, and the rest, as they say, is history. The dogs needed no introduction—Bow Tox was in doggie heaven from moment one.

Both couples now live together in Orlando and things are working out great. Dr. Larson often ponders what life would have been like if he had spent more time out of the office during those twenty-six years of practicing medicine. Who says Bow Tox doesn't lead to happiness?

Something's Fishy

Sharkey, as his friends liked to call him, was the son of a blue-collar father and a stay-at-home mom. His parents struggled every day to meet the basic needs for their three sons. Sharkey vowed to make something of himself, so that when he had a family of his own he could give his children more than he ever had.

True to his word, Sharkey worked hard all through high school to qualify for a scholarship to college. He majored in marine biology and graduated at the top of his class. He married Helena, his Romanian-born college sweetheart, shortly afterwards. His first job was his last—he'd been with the same marine research firm for almost 27 years. While he definitely worked his way up the ladder and provided for his family financially, he wasn't always there for them emotionally. He worked 14-hour days on the boat, putting in his time so he could show the owners that he had the dedication to be partner. Once partner, he thought he would be able to cut back his hours on the boat and work from home, growing the business and adding more boats to the fleet. Then he'd be able to spend some of his alone time fly-fishing, and any additional free time with Helena and the kids.

Somehow time got away from Sharkey, and before he knew it, so had his family. Both of Sharkey's sons were sports stars during their childhood and college years. His oldest son played baseball, while his youngest son, a huge Dolphins fan, played high school football. Even though the children played sports, performed in school plays, and sang in the church choir, he could count on one hand the number of times he attended those important events. There was always some deep-sea trip that came up unexpectedly and seemed like life-or-death at the time. He never realized that his family was also in need of his urgent attention, rationalizing in his own mind that he was working so hard for their benefit.

In the blink of an eye, Sharkey's sons were grown and off starting families of their own. A few years after their youngest son had left the nest, Helena was diagnosed with severe depression. She began taking prescription medication to deal with it. Her addiction grew, and after building up a tolerance for the prescribed stuff, she turned to some alternative methods. Sharkey was completely oblivious to all of this. In a wild string of events, Helena was arrested for possession of an illegal substance with intent to distribute and "sent up the river" for five years.

Almost overnight, Sharkey's life changed forever. Instead of spending his retirement years with his wife, traveling and enjoying his free time, Sharkey spent most of his days in front of the television napping and most of his nights eating TV dinners alone at the kitchen table. Because work was his life over the years, he had never taken the time to build relationships with his family or to make friends.

He barely saw his children, and his grandchildren only knew him from photos that Helena had sent to them when she was well. He called his sons and left messages, but most of his calls went unreturned. His kids were too busy with their own lives now to worry about him. When Sharkey was able to reach one of them by phone, it was usually a quick and stilted conversation. Since he hardly knew his sons and his sons hardly knew him, there wasn't much to talk about. Their conversations sounded more like those of strangers than family. When Sharkey sat alone in his easy chair his mind would wander back to the days when he thought that his career was the most important thing in his life. Now he had to admit that being a dad and husband—something he'd taken for granted—was more important than he'd ever realized.

Me, Myself, and Marcy

Marcy was a successful corporate lawyer who worked for a large financial institution in New York City. She burned the midnight oil on more than one occasion and was on a first name basis with the firm's cleaning crew. Her success earned her a fat salary, a bonus bigger than what most people earn in a year, and a corner office with a breathtaking view. Marcy had reached every career goal she had ever set for herself.

Marcy hit the gym every morning at 5:00 AM. She had a body that most girls dreamed of and every guy noticed. Exercise was critical for keeping her mind sharp and maintaining the stamina she needed to work all those long hours. She was also well aware that attractive people were more successful in business—like it or not, that's how it was.

To her coworkers, Friday night meant the end of the workweek and two days of relaxation with family and friends. Marcy had no weekends. Work was her life. If not in the office on Saturday, she was busy with laundry, clothes shopping, reading the latest trade journals, and planning out her gym schedule.

She had it all, didn't she? She was rich, accomplished in business, and beautiful. What else could someone want out of life?

On Marcy's fortieth birthday, she woke up by herself, like every other morning. She made a beeline for the gym, showered, and got dressed. Coffee in one hand and her briefcase in the other, she headed off to work. As she was walking into her office building, she noticed something that she normally would have ignored altogether. A mother bent down on one knee to wipe the crumbs off the face of her two-year-old. At that moment, Marcy's life flashed in front of her eyes and she felt her biological clock pounding through her blouse.

"Holy s—t, I'm 40! What have I done?"

She had always thought she would get married and have children someday. It always seemed to be something she would get to later. "Let me build my career and then take a break to start a family," she'd always said to herself. At that moment, she felt as unaccomplished in life as anyone can feel.

Professional Perspective

There is undoubtedly some sort of connection between fiscal fitness and happiness. Surely private housekeepers, yachts, and Mercedes parked in the garage can't be all bad. Money can provide comfort and pleasure, and these are certainly aspects of happiness. But when does the pursuit of comfort and pleasure start to undermine the happiness it is supposed to bring about?

All too often we are consumed with praising the false idol of money. While ideally your relationship with your career should be meaningful, what ultimately is the purpose of work? For most people, working provides a living and a sense of accomplishment, not necessarily a lifelong partner. People derive different types of satisfaction from their various roles in life. The challenge is to find a balance between those different roles.

David, Marcy, and Sharkey didn't make that happen. In David's case, his dedication to his career cost him his family, his friends, and his social skills. Once he gave up his practice he had to rebuild his personal connections with the human world. Whether they are with friends, family, or romantic partners, relationships are key assets in our lives, no less important (and often much more important) than financial assets.

Sharkey got so caught up in his career that he never really engaged with his family and their activities. Although he may have provided financially for them, the reality was that he didn't give them the kind of love and support they most likely wanted and needed. Now, after the fact, he may have a comfortable bank account but he has no one to enjoy its benefits with him.

Marcy, too, made great sacrifices in her personal life. She achieved financial independence, but realized when it was almost too late that she missed having children and someone with whom to create a family.

The ideal—difficult to achieve but very worth working toward—is a balance between goals in both work and personal life.

An important point to make here is that the definition of a successful personal life is a very individual one. For some it includes a spouse and children. For some it may center around involvement in community service. For others, religion is primary. What works for one person may not work for another.

These are just three scenarios of people who have lost track of what may really be important—human relationships. We can all tell stories of those people who have gotten caught up in working for the sake of a bigger house, bigger car, fancier clothes, thinking that those things will make them happy. In my opinion, happiness is not waking up alone, surrounded by expensive things, with no one to share your successes or your failures.

In the end, finding a balance between your personal and professional life may be the greatest accomplishment of all. Wealth is measured in more than one way.

Till Death (or Divorce) Do Us Part

"Forty for you, sixty for me. And equal partners we will be."

-Joan Rivers-

In La-La Land

By day Jessica was a successful, disciplined executive, planning product launches and handling a multimillion dollar budget. By night she was an idealist, wearing her heart on her sleeve and believing in the best in everyone. Her family and friends were very protective of her and were ready to fight off any guy that tried to take advantage of her trusting nature. When Jessica was in her early thirties she met Tyler, a doctor already established in a private practice.

Everyone always knew Tyler would be a successful doctor. He was intelligent, ambitious, and outgoing, and had a great rapport with his patients. His practice was growing fast and he'd recently moved his offices to a more desirable location with enough room so that he could bring in more state-of-the-art equipment as well as additional partners.

Everyone who met Jessica and Tyler thought the two were a perfect match. Nobody was surprised when they announced their engagement.

Jessica threw herself into planning the wedding with the same zeal she brought to a product launch. Tyler could hardly contain himself, either. At work, he kept sending her emails with names and addresses of cousins twice removed, former uncles by marriage, the brother of an ex-roommate's girlfriend, and the guys from his college ultimate Frisbee team. He wondered if they could get *two* bands and a DJ, so there would be different kinds of music at the reception.

As the guest list expanded, the potential venue grew larger, and the cost of the wedding seemed to grow exponentially. Neither Jessica nor Tyler minded—they were only planning on doing this once in their lives! "And after all," Tyler pointed out one night when they were going over the list, "that's why credit cards were invented." Jessica laughed, but then she saw that he wasn't joking.

"You think we should put the whole wedding expense on our credit cards?" she asked.

"Why not? It doesn't make a lot of difference, in my case. I financed the expansion of my practice with credit cards, and I'm still paying the interest on that. A little wedding debt is icing on the cake."

When Jessica met her best friends for drinks a few days later, she happened to mention Tyler's credit card situation. They were troubled, and told her so, but she wasn't worried. "We're going to be sharing everything we have for the rest of our lives," she said. "Anyway, I'm sure he knows what he's doing."

Strictly Business

Both Allen and Rachel were well established in their careers when they met. He was an attorney and she was a scientist. They were serious about their careers and life in general. When they were getting to know each other, they were amazed at how compatible their philosophies of life, money, family, and responsibility were. Not believing in leaving anything to chance, they had career plans established by 18, financial plans well in place by the time they were 28, and family plans now ready to be implemented.

Neither had the time nor interest to handle the details of planning their wedding. After interviewing several wedding planners they hired one that they were confidant could handle the planning independently. The wedding planner was given a detailed notebook of requirements, lists of guests with addresses, a budget, and told to contact them only in an emergency. The wedding planner had never worked with any couple so businesslike about their wedding. Although she dreaded the overly involved emotional types, this seemed to be very cold.

Now that the planning of the wedding could be checked off of their to-do list, Allen and Rachel moved on to the next item. They needed to discuss their financial lives. Each had investment portfolios, real estate, and, of course, checking accounts. Neither was eager to give the other the control of their combined finances. Each had been managing his or her own finances successfully for too long to be willing to cede control to the other.

After a lot of thought, they decided not to merge their finances at all. After all, they were getting married to start a family. Why did that mean they had to hold all their financial assets jointly? They came up with a plan that included buying a house as a partnership, dividing the bills between them and paying their share out of their individual checking accounts, and leaving their past as well as future investments in separate brokerage accounts.

Professional Perspective

Marriage means merging two individual people into a couple. The details of how this is done are very different from one couple to another. There is no right or wrong way to go about it as long as both people agree. The merging of financial lives is no different from the merging of other aspects of living.

Here are some of the most basic questions that need to be addressed:

- How are the routine bills going to get paid? Will you do it together or is one person going to be responsible?

- How are the bigger investment decisions going to be made? This may include anything from decisions about how *much* to invest, to *how* to invest it, to how to monitor your investments.

- Are you going to set up a household budget? How are you going to track actual spending?

- How do you feel about owing money? Do you carry credit card balances? Do you have a car payment or a lease payment? Are you so against owing money that you don't even want a mortgage? What if one of you has large debts and the other does not?

There is an underlying source of conflict in many of the above issues. Most of us have financial personality types. Whether we are spenders or savers, risk-takers or risk-averse investors, hands-on or totally hands-off, these are personality traits that either are hard-wired or have developed as a result of our upbringings. Joining two people with the individual baggage of twenty-something years or more and not expecting there to be issues is unrealistic. You'll have to address the all-important questions of Designated Dishwasher and

Acceptable Levels of Clutter, so expect the same mutual scrutiny of your financial personalities.

Some people, like Jessica in our first story, are totally trusting and naïve, never expecting that there could be problems down the road. For her, the thought of divorce is utterly foreign, and therefore she doesn't need to think ahead about a possible division of assets. The fact that her husband-to-be's financial judgment seems to lag far behind his medical skill, however, might suggest to someone of a less trusting disposition than Jessica the desirability of a prenuptial agreement.

A prenuptial agreement (or *prenup*) is a legal document drawn up prior to marriage that details how a couple's life will be divided up in the event of divorce. The exact contents of the contract will be different for each couple, but typically a prenup details how both assets and debts will be divided up, how inheritances will be dealt with, how future earnings will be handled, etc. A prenup is not only for the rich and famous. It can be a way to avoid the nastiness of an ongoing battle in the event of a divorce. Or, it can be useful if one or both parties expect a high level of future earnings or come into the marriage with extensive assets.

There is no right or wrong when it comes to a prenup. It is something that both parties have to agree to. For some, the decision is easy—maybe they see it as a logical business decision. For some, a prenup is something awful that takes all the love and romance out of getting married.

As I said earlier, we all come into marriage with baggage. Maybe one of our parents was a big spender and we listened to arguments when the credit card bills came in. Maybe we lived through a nasty divorce and want to protect ourselves. Maybe one of us grew up poor and financial security is critical. Some of us are better at meeting deadlines and scheduling routine tasks while some of us have never been good at keeping track of the bills. All of these things can make meshing financial lives difficult, but working through the issues will make for a happier marriage and a better chance of combined financial success.

It's Not a Tumor

"The only thing money gives you is the freedom of not worrying about money."

-Johnny Carson-

Richard had been our client almost since the first day the firm opened its doors. His account was in the seven-figure range. He lived on $40,000 a year and most of that came from his pension and Social Security. Bottom line, he didn't need to worry about money. However, he was very involved in making decisions about how his money was invested. He wasn't overly involved to the point that it was annoying, but he definitely kept his finger on the pulse of his account and investment activity. Speaking of pulses, did I mention that Richard had reached the ripe old age of 87?

While his health certainly was not the best, Richard managed to keep in touch with me even during times when he wasn't feeling so great. He had been in the office one late afternoon on a Friday so that we could review his portfolio performance. He had an accumulation of cash sitting in the account from a bond that was called the prior week and he was here now so we could discuss the options for investing that money. I told him about a short term private mortgage note that I felt would be suitable for him and his investment objectives. He said he wanted to think about it a little over the weekend and would get back to me by noon on Monday.

Monday morning came and went, and when I glanced at the clock it was nearly 3:15 PM. I hadn't heard from Richard, so I asked my assistant to place a quick phone call to his house. No answer, and no answering machine or voicemail. I felt a small pang in the pit of my stomach, but nudged it off. He was probably out at the grocery store or running some errand. Monday came to a close and so did Tuesday and Wednesday with no word from Richard. Even if he weren't interested in a recommendation, by now he normally would at least have called to let me know. This time—nothing.

On Thursday morning the situation became all too clear. I didn't hear from Richard himself, but I did hear from Richard's 60-year-old daughter, Joyce. On Sunday evening she had found Richard unconscious in his backyard. He'd been rushed to the hospital. I told her how sorry I was to hear that, but I was still a bit confused as to why she was calling me. She said that when her father regained consciousness after three days, the first words he managed to pronounce were, "Please make sure you tell Stu I am interested in that mortgage note and I'm sorry I didn't get back to him sooner!"

Professional Perspective

I must admit I sighed a little in exasperation when I heard those words. Worth more than $1 million and 87 years old, Richard's focus was on his money and not his health. His priorities were a little off base, to say the least. You just can't teach an old dog new tricks!

Paying too much attention to your money and investments is just as bad as investing and then ignoring your portfolio. There are times in everyone's life when investment decisions need to be put on the back burner while attention is paid to other things. A major health issue certainly qualifies as something that needs to take priority.

For the average investor, there are few times, if any, that an investment decision needs to be made immediately. Stock prices fluctuate from day to day and a bond may only be available for a short time, but another investment choice is most likely available. Something like a margin call may come that needs to be addressed immediately, but otherwise thinking about an investment for a few days before acting on it may be a prudent approach anyway.

On the other hand, there are arrangements that should be set up in advance in the event that a crisis diverts your attention for a period of time. Legal and medical documents will be discussed in a later chapter. Some of the simpler things that you should do include the following:

- **Ensure that someone has signatory authority for your checking account.** In the event you are incapacitated for a period of time, you want someone to be able to take care of paying your bills. There is nothing more stressful than recuperating with overdue notices, late payment fees, and threats to shut off your electricity for nonpayment.

- **Discuss with your financial advisor how much trading authority you want to give him or her.** You shouldn't have to worry about making investment decisions on the spot; on the other hand, you don't want to neglect your investments either.

- **Make sure a trusted family member or friend knows where your important items and contact phone numbers are located.** This person should be able to find your checkbook; a long-term care insurance policy, and car insurance policy if you've been in a car accident; and even something as simple as a mailbox key. The use of a "personal vault" will also be discussed in a later chapter (see "For the Organizationally Challenged").

- **Make certain**—as difficult a discussion as it may be—**your family knows whom you have designated to take charge of your affairs.** The middle of a crisis is no time for your adult children to hash out their own issues instead of properly and quickly taking care of the things that need to get done. Sometimes the choice is easy and logical, such as when only one child lives close by. Sometimes it may be more practical to designate a third party to handle these matters.

Proper planning will eliminate some of life's major stresses should a crisis, such as an illness, occur. All the other financial issues that we contend with are important, but not as important as health and family.

Those Were the Best Days of My Life

"I want my children to have all the things I couldn't afford.
Then I want to move in with them."

-Phyllis Diller-

Rob was the typical All American quarterback. You know the type: the high school football star with the cheerleader girlfriend on his arm, the guy who spends the rest of his life reliving those few months when the world revolved around him. He loved catching up with his buddies and rehashing the games play-by-play. In their undefeated senior year, he led his team to the state championship. All of the top football college scouts were at that game, and Rob knew this was his time. The 17–14 come-from-behind victory most likely secured his scholarship to Syracuse. Although Rob never started a game for the Orangemen, his college football days were a highlight of his life. First-string or third-string, football players were always big men on campus.

When Rob found out his wife Alicia was pregnant with their first child he was elated. Around twenty weeks into the pregnancy, Alicia had her first sonogram. Rob was by her side with his fingers crossed. The doctor said, "Congratulations, your son is coming along well." It took a second to register. Did he just say "son"? Rob almost hit the ceiling. That same day, he read through all the ads in his monthly alumni magazine and bought an Orangeman baby bib, baby bottle, and all the other Syracuse paraphernalia that could possibly clothe or catch the eye of a little boy destined for athletic greatness. His son would experience the adrenaline rush of running through the tunnel onto the field in front of 60,000 screaming fans. Rob daydreamed about his son being carried off the field on his teammates' shoulders, the blinding flashbulbs, the adulation, and the sea of orange and blue.

Fast-forward eighteen years.

Rob, his wife Alicia, and his son Kyle were all seated in my office. Rob had been banging his head against the wall trying to figure out where he was going to come up with the money to pay for the tuition, books, and housing for Kyle's college education. Rob had come to the realization five years ago that despite his constant coaching and encouragement, his son's football genes came from Alicia's side of the family. Though no one said it, I got the picture. There would be no football scholarship.

Alicia pointed out that Kyle had a gift for architecture and was interested in going to one of the top design schools in New York. The only scholarship hope now lay on the strength of his academics and his draftsmanship.

Professional Perspective

Although we all have ideas of what we hope our children will accomplish, at some point comes the realization that their lives and their dreams are their own. Ultimately, they have to do what they want to do. The right college for our children should be based on the right fit for them, not our attempts to relive our own glory days.

There are many factors to consider in choosing a college—everything from climate to setting (urban vs. secluded campus) to size to religious affiliation to the availability of specific programs, as in our example of the budding architect Kyle.

The college application process is filled with stress, paperwork, insecurity, and highs and lows. What we, as parents, can do is to try to plan ahead so that the final decision is not based on money. The final choice should be based on what school your child (not you) thinks is best for him or her.

The earlier parents can start saving, the better. Various parts of an investment plan can be put into place to take advantage of the remarkable power of compounding. Some of these tools may vary by state, and the pros and cons will vary depending on your state of residence. High school guidance counselors are also an excellent resource for information about college financial aid planning (e.g. grants, scholarships, federal and private loans, etc...). Some general information follows:

- Prepaid Plans—the basic premise of a prepaid plan is that, based upon the age of your child when you sign up and the plan type you sign up for, you prepay tuition, housing, etc., based on costs today. (Of course, your child still has to qualify academically for the school.) You are guaranteed to cover the costs when your child enrolls, no matter how much the cost of education and housing has risen. In Florida, this guarantee is for all Florida state universities and community colleges. The value can also be transferred to most private colleges in Florida as well as many out-of-state schools. The example below is for a child living in Florida of kindergarten age in 2006:

	Lump Sum Payment Plan	Monthly Payment Plan (Five Year)	Monthly Payment Plan (Ongoing)
Four-year tuition plan	$11,089.56	$220.24	$99.48
Two plus two tuition plan	$9,034.44	$179.44	$81.05
Two-year tuition plan	$3,529.07	$69.91	$31.58

http://www.florida529plans.com

- 529 Plans—investments made in a 529 plan (the 529 refers to a section of the tax code) grow tax deferred. When they are withdrawn for qualified college expenses, they are exempt from federal income taxes. Many states offer 529 plans, each one with different investment vehicles to pick from. What is best for you will vary based on investment performance, state tax issues, administrative costs, and other factors.[1]

- Parent Loan for Undergraduate Students—PLUS loans are available for parents and are not need-based. They have a low, variable interest rate that has a cap. There are also various repayment plans available. Depending on a family's individual set of circumstances this may be a viable option to consider.

College is a unique time of life. It's one of the only times you experience work, study, and play all at the same time and in the same place. It's also a bizarre time—isn't it strange that an eighteen-year-old kid, perhaps at a moment of weakness, may very well determine how you live the rest of your life? Ideally, each person should have the opportunity to have his or her own chosen experience at this stage of life. Our job as parents is to help guide our children through the admission process and plan our finances so that they have as many options available to them as possible.

Life Planning—Quick Recap

Couples

- Financial planning sometimes requires the same level of communication—and the same degree of honesty—as marriage counseling.

Balance

- Relationships are key assets in our lives.

- The definition of a successful personal life is an individual one.

- Balance between personal and professional life is difficult, but striving for that balance may be the most important thing you do.

The Marriage Merger

- Most of us have financial personality types. It might take some adjustment for those personalities to mesh in a marriage.

- There's no single right way to combine assets and financial responsibilities in marriage—both sides just need to be comfortable with the situation.

- There can be sound reasons for wanting a prenuptial agreement regardless of how much money either person has. Of course, prenups are not everyone's idea of a romantic wedding preparation.

Priorities

- There are times in everyone's life when investment decisions need to be put on the back burner.

- Paying too much attention to your money and investments is just as bad as investing and then ignoring your portfolio.

- For the average investor, there are few times, if any, that an investment decision needs to be made immediately.

- It's vitally important to make arrangements in advance for what to do with your finances in the event of a health crisis.

Saving for College

- Children need to pick the school that's best for them, not the school their parents have fantasized about them going to.

- The goal for parents is to plan ahead so that the final decision about where their children will attend college is not based on money.

- There are several different investment strategies for parents who want to start saving early for their children's education. The best fit depends on where you live and what your circumstances are.

INVESTMENT MANAGEMENT

"The sports car and sailboat are investments for my retirement. I'm using them to attract a younger woman who can support me in my old age."

Analysis Paralysis

"I've had great success being a total idiot."

-Jerry Lewis-

Scott worked in the high tech industry as an engineer. He was married and had two children. His wife stopped working when their second child was born but planned on going back to work at some point. Scott took his role as provider for the family very seriously.

Perhaps not surprisingly for an engineer, Scott was very detail-oriented and accustomed to sifting through and analyzing a lot of data. He was a very methodical sort of guy at work, and in other parts of his life, too. As soon as he was eligible, he stopped by the Human Resource department to find out about the company's 401(k) plan. The HR manager handed him a packet of material to read and told him he needed to fill out the necessary forms to enroll in the retirement plan.

The 401(k) plan had 14 different investment options to choose from. Other than reading the headlines in the business section of the local paper and tuning in to CNBC periodically, Scott wasn't very knowledgeable about finance—but he felt he was intelligent and could learn. The booklets indicated that the investments varied by risk. Scott was very comfortable doing research on the Internet. He decided he would start gathering data on each of the investment options available to him. He figured he would apply the same type of methodology he used at work. This would lead him to make the best investment decisions for him and his family.

He set up a folder for each possible investment. Each evening after the kids went to bed, Scott sat down at his computer to gather data. The closer the deadline came for the forms to go into the Human Resource Department, the more the folders filled with the fruits of his research. Scott became more and more apprehensive about having to make the decision. After all, his family was depending on him. Night after night Scott kept digging for more data, more analysis, that final piece of information that would make the decision clear to him.

Three months later, Scott was still not enrolled in the 401(k) plan. He had beaten himself up so much over not being able to make a decision that his work was suffering. He put the folders aside one night and figured he would revisit the research when things calmed down at work and his mind was a little clearer.

During those three months, the markets had the biggest rally in the past twenty years. Scott was beside himself. He'd missed a once-in-a-lifetime opportunity. What should he do now? If he enrolled today, he would be buying at an all-time high, a horrible decision he was not going to make. The market rallied for another six months and Scott had trouble looking in the mirror. Where could he go from here?

Professional Perspective

Everyone has a different investing personality type. Some people would rather delegate everything to their financial advisor and not be involved in any of the decision-making. To them, a quarterly summary report and an annual meeting are plenty. Others think of investing more like a sport and a pastime. To them, the process is as much fun as the result—they want in on all the action. Most of us fall someplace in the middle.

No matter how much or little we would like to be involved, many of us are being forced into taking a much more active role in our investing strategy and retirement planning than did previous generations. As more companies implement defined contribution plans (401(k)'s), fewer and fewer people today have traditional defined benefit (pension) plans. It has become increasingly apparent that we now have to take responsibility for our own financial well being. The days of working for a firm for our entire career and trusting the company to take care of us in retirement are behind us.

Not only are we being forced to make decisions about investment options within our 401(k)'s, but we also know we need to invest beyond that in order to have a sound financial future. At the same time that the investing and retirement planning world is changing, the Internet has grown explosively. In the past, the average person didn't have access to the vast amount of data available today. Added to the mix is the fact that the curriculum offered to our students has not really kept pace with these changes. People are not being educated about basic realities of personal finance today. The result is that the majority of investors really don't have the tools to make smart decisions.

Many of us are like Scott. Unsure of how to make the best investment decision, we keep hunting for that piece of information that will guarantee that we're making the right choice. Unfortunately, there is no final piece to the puzzle. But the worst thing an investor can do in this situation is nothing. For 401(k) investors, doing nothing means not only that they are not investing their own money, but also that they're foregoing the matching contribution their employer may make.

Websites like MarketWatch, Motley Fool, and SmartMoney are full of information about the economy, firms, funds, and trends. CNBC covers the markets all day long. There are many valuable tools to use in the decision-making process but, in the final analysis, you eventually need to fight off paralysis and make the best choices you can. Sometimes your gut is your best guide.

Buy High, Sell Low

"October: This is one of the particularly dangerous
months to invest in stocks. Other dangerous months are
July, January, September, April, November, May, March,
June, December, August, and February."

-Mark Twain-

Joe Weinstock, a tightly wound ball of stress, tiptoed into the conference room for his first meeting. A time bomb waiting to explode, he was shaky and anxious and clearly on edge. I assumed he was either a drug addict or on the verge of a nervous breakdown—maybe both. I was right on the second count anyway.

Standing five feet five inches tall, a mildly successful computer programmer originally from Michigan, Joe was the fourth of eight children. Intellectually acute but socially inept, he was plagued by his constant need for reassurance.

At the office Joe was a shy guy, a follower. He would often stop to chat with coworkers at the water cooler in hopes of finding a friend. He would overhear Larry Carey and Melony Felony discussing their victorious investments and he couldn't help feeling envy. These were the conversations that led Joe to dabble in the stock market on the side. Unfortunately, he was not destined for success.

Time and again he would buy at market highs only later to suffer severe lows. His stock picks were generally chosen based on the previous year's performance; timing was his downfall.

Soon Joe found himself obsessively watching his stocks. He became irrational and distraught. As soon as he woke up he would turn on the TV to CNBC, hanging on every word of the financial analysts while downing cups of black coffee. As his coworkers bragged about their earnings, Joe quietly sank into a depression.

Now six months later and twenty thousand dollars poorer, Joe sat before us seeking guidance. Nearly in tears, he gripped his cup of water and told us that he had lost money he couldn't afford to lose. I tried to console him with well-worn anecdotes, but there was nothing I could say at that moment to alleviate his distress.

Forty-five minutes went by before Joe could gather his emotions. This was when my partner and I proceeded to sift through the paperwork of Joe's remaining funds. I purposely made positive remarks about the potential upsides to what was left in his portfolio, as this was obviously a sensitive situation. I decided that we should meet one week later to discuss his financial future in detail. Joe grinned appreciatively and he packed his briefcase.

One week later Joe walked out of the conference room with his chin lifted a bit higher than the week before. My partner had presented him with a portfolio recommendation that was far more conservative in comparison to Joe's prior investment dealings, but which would place him on much sounder footing for the years to come. Again there were tears at the corners of Joe's eyes, but this time they were tears of relief.

Two years have since gone by and Joe has found golf to be the best bonding method with his coworkers. He now focuses solely on computer programming and happily leaves financial investing decisions to someone else.

Professional Perspective

A common way that people choose their investments is by basing their decision solely on the previous year's performance. Joe Weinstock is a classic example of a do-it-yourselfer. It is not unusual for an investor to look at last year's best performer and decide to buy it. I generally refer to this as the "bandwagon" syndrome, where individuals will buy something because everyone else already did.

At the same time, investors also tend to prematurely sell their worst performing investment of that year, never giving it the opportunity to have its best year.

Purchasing based on proven performance is not necessarily wrong; however, the selection process should be researched and discussed. Investments operate a little differently from most other purchases and they are not to be taken lightly.

For instance, if you were to buy a car, you might study industry reports that rate the best car in a given class, according to price, safety, gas mileage, etc. You should be applauded for that kind of research. It wouldn't be prudent to walk into a dealership and buy a car spontaneously without having any idea of what to expect under the hood or on the road.

When purchasing an investment, you would want to know more than just last year's performance and which investment was "best in its class." Your other considerations could be 3-year, 5-year, and 10-year track records, as well as risk/reward statistical measures. After all, the greater an investment's possible reward over time, generally the greater its level of price volatility, or risk.

Further research will crystallize in your mind the unlikelihood that the investment that performed best last year will again be the top performer (**see illustration**). Investment asset classes go through cycles. (Investment asset classes being large growth type companies, small value-oriented companies, mid-size growth oriented companies, etc.) While not always the case, it is not unusual for the worst performing asset class the prior year to be the best (or near best) performing asset class in the current year.

rank	1998	1999	2000	2001	2002	2003	2004	2005
1	Russell 1000 Growth 38.71%	S&P/IFC G Emerging Markets 62.72%	LB Agg 11.63%	LB Agg 8.44%	LB Agg 10.25%	S&P/IFCG Emerging Markets 54.44%	S&P/IFC G Emerging Markets 27.64%	S&P/IFC G Emerging Markets 41.83%
2	S&P 500 28.58%	Russell 1000 Growth 33.16%	Russell 1000 Value 7.01%	CG 3-Month T Bill 4.09%	CG 3-Month T Bill 1.70%	Russell 2500 45.51%	MSCI EAFE 20.25%	MSCI EAFE 13.54%
3	MSCI EAFE 20.00%	MSCI EAFE 26.96%	CG 3-Month T Bill 5.96%	Russell 2500 1.22%	S&P/IFCC Emerging Markets -5.64%	MSCI EAFE 38.59%	Russell 2500 18.29%	Russell 2500 8.11%
4	Russell 1000 Value 15.63%	Russell 2500 24.15%	Russell 2500 4.27%	S&P/IFCG Emerging Markets -0.29%	Russell 1000 Value -15.52%	Russell 1000 Value 30.03%	Russell 1000 Value 16.49%	Russell 1000 Value 7.05%
5	LB Agg 8.69%	S&P 500 21.04%	S&P 500 -9.10%	Russell 1000 Value -5.59%	MSCI EAFE -15.94%	Russell 1000 Growth 29.75%	S&P 500 10.88%	Russell 1000 Growth 5.26%
6	CG 3-Month T Bill 5.05%	Russell 1000 Value 7.35%	MSCI EAFE -14.17%	S&P 500 -11.89%	Russell 2500 -17.80%	S&P 500 28.68%	Russell 1000 Growth 6.30%	S&P 500 4.91%
7	Russell 2500 0.38%	CG 3-Month T Bill 4.74%	Russell 1000 Growth -22.42%	Russell 1000 Growth -20.42%	S&P 500 -22.10%	LB Agg 4.10%	LB Agg 4.34%	CG 3-Month T Bill 3.00%
8	S&P/IFCG Emerging Markets -21.09%	LB Agg -0.82%	S&P/IFC G Emerging Markets -28.77%	MSCI EAFE -21.44%	Russell 1000 Growth -27.88%	CG 3-Month T Bill 1.07%	CG 3-Month T Bill 1.24%	LB Agg 2.43%

These eight indices represent broad asset classes. As you can see by tracking them over the past eight years, the performance of an asset class can change dramatically from year to year.

The jury is still out on the overall benefit of do-it-yourself investors having such ready access to all kinds of information regarding these investments. Average consumers like Joe are not equipped to decipher the data in order to make intelligent decisions. They are presented with historical results, expert opinions (which change sometimes on a daily basis), and graphs up the wazoo. But what does it all mean? Since every investor's situation is different, how can anyone decide what is the best option?

Due at least in part to the discipline financial advisors can bring to investing (avoiding emotional buying and selling), it is widely asserted that investors who work through a financial representative typically outperform do-it-your-selfers, thereby justifying the added cost of hiring the right help. Working with an advisor does not by any means assure you of success. However, the value added may be in the advice that minimizes your losses in any given year or keeps you from shooting yourself in the foot. Sometimes the greatest benefit I provide my clients is saving them from themselves.

Five Fund Sally

"There's no business like show business, but there are
several businesses like accounting."

-David Letterman-

Sally was a thirty-five year old single woman who had made it through the first two years of college but never finished her degree. She started working at a finance company as a secretary for the office manager, and over the years had managed to work her way up into the Accounts Receivable Supervisor position in the corporate headquarters of the firm. She had learned some things over the years from her coworkers and bosses. She did what she thought was necessary to stay abreast of current market conditions by reading the *Wall Street Journal* every morning and subscribing to an investment site online that updated her on any changes in her current portfolio via email.

Sally thought she had sufficient education to invest her money. She decided to put her cash savings into five different mutual funds that were all part of one mutual fund family. She had thoroughly researched the funds by reading about the fund managers, analyzing graphs of past performance of the funds, and even looking up what the fund managers had done in the past to replace stocks that weren't performing up to par within the fund. She was confident that she had done enough research to make an educated decision.

Sally continued to follow her funds in the financial newspapers and magazines. When she saw ads for a few of them she was pleased to see that they had been given 5-star ratings by Morningstar, Inc. At the end of the quarter she saw that many of the publications ran lists of the largest (ranked by asset size) mutual funds and the returns for various time frames. She nearly broke her arm patting herself on the back when she saw several of her funds on these lists. Two years later, however, gravity flexed its muscle—what goes up must come down. All five funds that experienced simultaneous growth experienced simultaneous decline.

Professional Perspective

Sally did all of this research based on what she read was the right thing to do, but in reality she had no idea what all of the information she had compiled really meant. While she had chosen five different mutual funds, all of the funds were from the same mutual fund company, which isn't necessarily a problem.

However, just because they were all quality funds that performed well doesn't mean they were the right combination of funds for her.

Unfortunately for Sally, the five funds she had chosen to invest in contained many of the same stocks. In other words, Sally didn't have a truly diversified portfolio. She had invested her money in what she thought were five completely different funds. But the fact that many of the funds had the same investment objectives meant that they were choosing from the same universe of companies. Sally had good intentions, but her good intentions didn't help her to meet her goal because she'd ended up doing exactly what she was trying to avoid in the first place—putting all her eggs in one basket.

To prove this point, we examined the top ten holdings in six funds randomly selected from among the most popular large-cap growth funds. Five funds held Microsoft, five funds held General Electric, four funds held AIG, four funds held Wal-Mart, four funds held Intel, and four funds held Lowe's. If you had chosen several of these well-known funds to invest in, potentially half of their major positions would have overlapped.

Not only is this an issue with funds that have similar investment objectives, but also the large mutual fund companies have multiple funds with similar investing objectives. There is nothing wrong with investing in multiple funds within a fund family, but you need to be aware of the investing style of each of the funds.

One way to avoid this situation is to use Morningstar's Style Box[2]. It categorizes investments on two main variables: size of the firms the fund can invest in and whether they are growth- or value-oriented companies. Separate Style Boxes can be used for domestic funds and international funds.

Small, medium, and large refers to the market capitalization (the total value of a company's stock) of the firm. In 2006, **large caps** have a market capitalization of greater than $5 billion, **medium caps** have a market capitalization of $1 to $5 billion, and **small caps** have a market capitalization of less than $1 billion.

Value-oriented investments are in companies that are considered undervalued based upon fundamental measures. The goal is to find and invest in those companies before their price per share catches up with their profitability. **Growth-oriented** investments are in companies that are experiencing revenue and earnings growth. The assumption is that the stock price will grow as the company's revenue and earnings grow.

Mutual Fund Style Box

Morningstar, Inc.

Trying to choose investments that use different criteria may help reduce the chances of investing in multiple investments holding the same stocks. Although categorizing investments is in some cases a judgment call, and some really don't fall cleanly into one category or another, determining styles is a starting point in deciding what to invest in.

A financial advisor has access to a vast amount of data that you may either not have access to or not want to plow your way through. By taking advantage of your advisor's knowledge and guidance in this process, you may avoid unknowingly investing in the same thing many times over.

Fishing Rod

"Money was never a big motivation for me, except as a way
to keep score. The real excitement is playing the game."

-Donald Trump-

Rod loved to fish for dolphin and also for great business investment opportunities. Rod's number one source of bait was his "buddy" Sam. Sam was forever coming across these harebrained business ideas and "sure thing" investment opportunities for them to sink their money in. Rod and Sam had known each other since they were in elementary school, and Rod had always followed Sam's advice.

Rod actually had a stable job with a steady and sizeable income, so his financial situation had allowed him to invest in several of Sam's golden opportunities. Unfortunately, most of the investments that Rod made based on Sam's urgings ended up being busts. He not only lost out on the profit he was supposed to reap in the future, but he also lost the money he initially put into the investments.

When Rod walked into our office, he had a folder clutched in his right hand that we soon came to know as the home of his bank and investment account statements. At first glance, I could see that he had lost quite a bit of money on a monthly basis due to various stock and mutual fund purchases. Looking back over the year's worth of bank statements, I noticed a couple of large checks that had been written to what seemed like numerous small companies I'd never heard of. When I asked Rod what the checks were written for, he launched into a ten-minute speech about various business investment opportunities that were supposed to lead him down the road to riches. He even told us that his friend Sam had just slipped him a tip about an up-and-coming company that was about to launch a new drink for the health conscious. It was expected to be a huge hit. In his next breath, he told us he was looking for a way to squeeze together $10,000 to help the drink company launch the product. He was preparing to tap into his six-figure 401(k) account to fund this next opportunity. He figured he was guaranteed to double his money in three months and quadruple his money by the end of the first year.

I sat there in amazement, watching the excitement flicker in Rod's eyes at the prospect of investing in yet another Sam "sure thing." Even though Rod came up empty over and over, he was actually in the process of throwing out his line again to see if this time he could catch the big one.

Professional Perspective

Why are we always looking for the next big kill? Most of us are savvy enough to avoid the really ludicrous get-rich-quick schemes. But we are always ready to listen to stories about how someone made a killing flipping condos, investing in penny stocks, or selling garage sale finds on eBay. The reality is that for every story we hear about someone who timed the tech bubble perfectly and is now a retired multi-millionaire at 40, there are hundreds of stories about people who have lost money through crazy investment schemes and bad timing.

Like those who seek out fast cars, extreme sports, or high stakes gambling, there are those investors who live for the thrill of the next big score, however farfetched it sounds. I wouldn't be surprised if brain chemistry is involved in the constant need some people have to put their money into these types of investments. But there is a way for them to satisfy this need without risking their savings in the process.

Based upon your individual circumstances, you may be able to allocate a certain amount of money for "mad money," which can be kept in a separate account and used for these types of long-shot investments. Your mad money fund should not have any impact on how much money you put away to achieve your long-term goals. This is not money you need to live on or plan your future with. If your mad money investment loses its entire value, it should be frustrating, maybe a little embarrassing, but not devastating.

The key principles of long term investing may not be sexy and exciting—and they may not make you the center of attention at a cocktail party—but they work. These principles include:

> **Dollar Cost Averaging**: a technique for investing a fixed dollar amount in an investment at regular intervals. When the price of the investment falls, more shares are purchased; when the price of the investment rises, fewer shares are purchased, thereby reducing the average cost per share of the investment. It also reduces the chance of buying an investment at a high price due to unlucky timing.

> **Reinvest your interest/dividends and capital gains.** While you are in your working and investing years, you can put the money you have earned on your investments to work for you by reinvesting it. Then, the money you

have earned is earning money for you—this is the principle of compounding.

For mutual funds, fees are almost as important as performance. Before you invest, make sure you research fees. A high fee structure will reduce your returns each year, thus putting less money to work for you over time. In addition to fees, pay attention to sales loads. Unless you expect to get service and advice from the financial representative, sales-loaded funds may not be cost effective. The value of advice is typically worth the price. However, there are many very good no-load mutual funds available so that all your initial investment gets invested. Please note that deferred sales charges may apply to redemptions/surrenders of no-load funds.

Hopefully, you'll find your adrenaline rush from something other than investing (although don't take this as your cue to start cliff diving!). If you can't help thrill seeking with your money, then put aside some mad money strictly for this use, but make sure your future goals can be met by other means. The strategy of "slow and steady wins the race" will get you to your financial finish line with a higher degree of success than going for the quick sprints and steep short cuts.

You Can't Handle the Risk

"You can't expect to hit the jackpot if you don't put a few nickels in the machine."

-Flip Wilson-

George was a take-charge type of guy, a do-it-yourselfer in every sense of the word. He had been an officer in the military and now was a construction project manager for a major homebuilder. He took on the role of troubleshooter at work and was able to dive into every problem that arose and figure out how to get the job done. He knew enough about each trade that he was able to successfully work with all the subcontractors. The projects George was overseeing came in on time and on budget.

George began investing in the stock market in the nineties. Every time he was around a group of people, all he heard about was how much money they were making in the stock market. (Seems to be a common theme....) He figured that if they could do it, so could he. After all, he was accustomed to attacking the problem at hand, figuring out what to do about it, implementing the solution, and then moving on to the next task.

For the next several months, George paid attention to the names of the stocks he heard everyone talking about. All those dot coms kept coming up and although he didn't really know much about Internet businesses or how the companies made money, they seemed to be the hot stocks. George started to buy the stocks and stash them away in his portfolio. Each month he'd look at the bottom line on his statement and think proudly about how he'd figured out this stock market thing without any professional help. This seemed to be the easiest sure bet out there.

Soon George had invested all his available money in the market and he turned his attention elsewhere. You can see where this is going. Before he realized what was happening, his stocks declined dramatically in value. They'd climbed quickly, but they fell even faster.

Before, he used to turn on CNBC as soon as he got home from work to catch up on the action of the day. Now, after a few days of watching how much the Dow and NASDAQ had gone down, he de-programmed CNBC from his remote control. He wondered what the Nielsen ratings for the channel were now compared to a few years ago.

Before, when his brokerage statements came in the mail he couldn't wait to read them. When they came now he left them on the kitchen counter for a few days while he worked up the courage to open them. Each time he'd pass the envelope on the counter his stomach would roll and his heart would pound. When he finally did open the envelope and look at the values, he'd feel sick and head straight for the bathroom. His young son was soon questioning why Daddy was "taking so many potty breaks."

George's confidence was shaken. For the first time in his life, he didn't know what he had done wrong, nor did he know what to do about it.

Professional Perspective

Everyone has their own definition of risk as well as their own perception of how much risk they can handle. While to some this account may sound like an overly dramatized version of reality, there are many of you reading this who think I'm telling your story. The reality of how much risk you can actually handle is usually very different from your perception.

The stock market of the late 1990s through 2002 is a dramatic case in point. A lot of people were simply unrealistic about how much risk they thought they could take. From new investors to more sophisticated veterans, everyone seemed to be lulled into an assumption that the stock market could only go up. Even when stocks began to decline, many people didn't sell—they felt that the market would rebound and there was more money to be made. Even the savviest of investors forgot some of the basic principles of investing, such as rebalancing their portfolios or diversifying their investments. They were subjecting themselves to levels of risk well beyond what they could handle emotionally.

Before you can define how much risk you can really handle in your portfolio without developing an ulcer, you have to have an understanding of the different facets of risk. Without sounding too much like a college finance textbook, **let's review some basics about risk.**

Many people think bonds are completely safe investments. In reality, bonds are subject to several types of risk: **interest rate risk** refers to the fact that the market price of a bond will decline if interest rates rise. Bonds with longer maturities tend to be more sensitive to changes in interest rates, usually making them more volatile than bonds with shorter maturities; **call risk** means that your bond may be called if interest rates decline and you aren't able to replace the level of interest; **inflation risk** refers to the risk you take if you buy a bond in an inflationary environment. The flat coupon rate may not keep pace with the increase in the cost of living. While some people may think they are being conservative by investing entirely in bonds, actually they are subjecting themselves to a fair degree of risk. For most bonds there is a risk that the issuer will default. Also, high-yield bonds generally are more susceptible to the risk of default than higher rated bonds.

Some people feel that the stock market is far too risky a gamble to be involved in. In fact, over time, the stock market has had higher returns than most other investment categories (e.g. bonds, cash). But, as George found, putting together a portfolio of stocks that will give you those returns isn't necessarily an easy thing to do.

Investing in young, volatile companies without a proven track record can result in high returns, but at great risk. Generally, the greater an investment's possible reward over time, the greater its level of price volatility, or risk. These aggressive types of investments can have a place in a portfolio but should not make up the portfolio as a whole. (However, adding high-risk investments may actually *decrease* the overall level of portfolio risk due to non-correlation of performance. In other words, these additional high risk investments may do well in periods when the rest of the equity markets are performing poorly, thereby offering some protection on the down side for your portfolio.) Many of the high-flying dot com companies of the 1990s went out of business without ever posting any earnings. The few that did survive, such as eBay, have given their investors great returns. An investor must assess the risks of the business and only invest as much as he or she is willing to lose. Please remember that past performance is no guarantee of future results.

A portfolio that is highly concentrated in one area—such as George's—is far riskier than a diversified portfolio. This is true even in mutual fund investing. There are funds that are balanced, meaning they are invested in stocks, bonds, and cash equivalents. These are fairly low risk but that does not mean no risk. On the other end of the spectrum are industry-specific sector funds, such as healthcare funds or technology funds. Because an industry tends to move together, these funds carry a greater than average risk (as well as a higher potential return) and are often more volatile than funds holding a diversified portfolio of stocks in many industries.

With risk comes the potential for stress. The goal is to put together a portfolio that is appropriate to meet your goals and that will let you sleep at night. Everyone has to address honestly how much risk he or she is willing to take. Understanding the risks associated with various types of investments is a start. The next step is to **decide how much risk you can handle.** Some questions to ask yourself include:

- Given that markets go up and markets go down (and they do!), what dollar value loss in a year can you handle emotionally? Think of it in terms of what you can actually do with that amount of money.

- If you can separate investments into short-term vs. long-term needs, can you handle more volatility in the long-term portion of your investments, understanding that portfolio values can go down in a one year time horizon?

- Are you going to watch the returns on your investments every day and agonize over every blip in the market?

- If you are a do-it-yourselfer, are you willing to put the time into research, follow-up, etc., in order to manage a volatile portfolio?

As George found out too late, putting together a high-flying, high-risk portfolio is fun to watch on the way up but is sickening to watch on the way down. Many people lost most of the value of their investments and had to change their lifestyles and their retirement plans. There are people now, six years into the new millennium, who are behaving in much the same way with real estate investing. They have taken out large home equity loans to finance other real estate purchases, are carrying interest-only mortgages, and are trying to buy and flip properties to make some quick money. Subjecting yourself to large amounts of risk doesn't only happen with the stock market—it can happen in any investment category.

A financial advisor will be able to help you assess your risk tolerance. But your financial advisor (or you, if you do it yourself) will only be able to put together the right kind of portfolio if you honestly define how much risk you are able to assume.

See No Evil, Hear No Evil

"The only way not to think of money is to have a great deal of it."

-Edith Wharton-

Wealthy, wildly successful, and happily unmarried, Alyson Potter was living it up on the Miami social scene. She grew up in nearby Boca Raton in a very wealthy family, typical for the area. Her father was a client of ours, a successful businessman and investor who played in real estate. Alyson took after her father—well, somewhat. She was certainly a risk taker.

A business executive by day and party girl by night, Alyson enjoyed her freedom. She was twenty-six years old with no man, no kids, and lots of money. In her mind she had no financial worries. She never looked at price tags, generously showered friends with gifts, and dangerously dabbled in stocks.

One Saturday night, Alyson was hanging out at the Delano Hotel in Miami when she met a striking dark-haired man. They sat and talked over drinks into the late hours. His name was Trevor and apparently was a hotshot broker with a trendy South Beach investment firm. His baby blue eyes and dimples fascinated her, so much so that she was hanging on his every word. He could have been discussing pork bellies and she would have bought it. In the course of their conversation she misguidedly happened to mention how well off her dad was and that her current investments were not performing up to snuff. Trevor took full advantage of the moment and walked away with a client and a date. He touted an IPO his firm was involved with and recommended she pick up 1,000 shares when it hit the market at $85 per share.

One month later, she got in at $120 per share. In two days, the stock was trading at $180. Alyson was too excited over her new relationship to give much thought to her stock. Her father, a shrewd businessman, did not share her sentiments about the man or the stock. However, he felt his daughter was old enough to make her own choices. When Trevor realized that Alyson's dad was not interested in becoming a client, he quickly ended the relationship. Alyson was too devastated to eat, let alone check the financial markets.

It took two weeks for her to crawl out of bed and join the world of the living. In those two weeks, the stock plummeted to $100 per share. Alyson considered buying more to lower her average cost basis, but decided to sit back and watch for another few days. By the end of that week, Alyson found herself with a stock worth $20, no broker, and no boyfriend.

Professional Perspective

When faced with an opportunity to buy or sell, many of us freeze and do nothing. That's the power of inertia. How many of us watched our investment portfolios decline from 2000 to 2002 and didn't lift a finger? Like Alyson, we find it easier not to act than to change. However, we have to realize that doing nothing is in itself a decision.

Granted, sitting tight and riding it out was for some of us a conscious, proactive decision. But most of us curled up in a ball, refused to open our brokerage account statements when they came in the mail each month, and prayed for better days.

Instead, we should have taken notice of what was happening, re-addressed our risk tolerance, and repositioned accordingly.

So why do we buy a stock, track it for a year, watch it appreciate in value, and then do nothing? Why can't we pull the trigger and take some profits?

The overriding message of this book is delivered in many different ways: the average person falls into a trap when he or she is unable to put emotion aside and buy and sell based on intellect and strict discipline. The key is not to get attached to the investment itself—and in the case of Alyson, not to the broker either. An investment is not a living and breathing thing. It is a means to an end.

Once you decide to purchase it, you need to establish a goal for that investment. Having the discipline to sell when that goal is reached (both on the gain and loss side) is a critical part of investing. We all tend to get greedy when an investment is doing well and we all tend to be in denial when an investment is doing poorly. By pre-establishing and re-evaluating positions, some of the emotion can be taken out of the equation.

We've been brainwashed into believing we shouldn't sell when our investments are down. If we wait things out maybe they'll come back! Well, my friends, we are in a different world now.

An investment like the stock Alyson purchased had no business being priced at $180 per share. It also had no business being priced at $120 per share. But we still kicked ourselves when we watched it jump from $120 to $180. Oh, the money we could have made if we only had pulled the trigger! Already, people were daydreaming of all the toys they were going to buy with their newfound wealth. Of course, their wealth was only on paper, and only lasted a short time. Until you sell, you haven't made any money.

When the price fell from $180 to $100 per share, we contemplated buying more. What a great buying opportunity. We may never see such a low price per share again. Then it dropped to $80 and we thought long and hard again. Imagine our average cost per share if we got in at the bargain basement price of $80.

Thank the stars for procrastination. There should have been no expectation that we would see $180 again in the next decade, if ever. For all the times we were burned by paralysis, immobilization sure came in handy this time. Yes, Alyson lost her investment but she could have continued to buy on the way down, throwing good money after bad.

Paralysis transcends the investment world. Decision-making in all areas of our life becomes more difficult during extreme circumstances. Sometimes doing nothing is the smart thing, as long as you acknowledge that you are choosing to do nothing instead of running scared and trying to avoid the responsibility of making a decision. As in Alyson's case, doing nothing and forgetting about your investments can have major consequences.

Off Balance

"As long as the world is turning and spinning, we're
gonna be dizzy and we're gonna make mistakes."

-Mel Brooks-

Everyone thought Tina was ditzy. The teachers in high school had little confidence in her abilities and never pushed her to do much in the way of schoolwork. She was a favorite of teacher and student alike, always upbeat and willing to pitch in and help out. But she was a little flaky. Her nickname was Teetering Tina—on the go in spike heel shoes, ready to dive into the next pep rally, party, or cause.

After high school she took some secretarial courses and then went to work for Prime Management, a young high tech company. It was a laid back type of business, but everyone was willing to do what was needed to get the job done and make the company a success. This was perfect for Tina. She found that she was good with the customers, her fellow workers appreciated her attitude and spirit, and no one held it against her that she hadn't gone to college.

Being a young company, Prime wasn't able to pay very high salaries but it was generous with stock options. The plan was that if everyone had a stake in trying to make Prime a success, they would be motivated to work harder.

Prime's management found that when they needed to get something done, Teetering Tina was there. Soon she was promoted from secretary to sales. It turned out that, though outwardly Tina might look ditzy with her spike heels, trendy clothes and blonde hair, on the inside she had a killer instinct. She knew how to close a deal. People loved her and she somehow knew how to approach each potential customer.

As Prime grew, so did the amount of Prime stock that Tina held. She paid no attention to this at all; she was young and enjoying her successes. Her financial future and retirement were just not on her mind. She was now their top sales person and supervised several of the new hires. Prime rewarded her with some generous options at the end of each year.

Soon Prime decided that it was time to offer their employees a 401(k) with matching contributions. Tina signed up right away and didn't spend much time worrying about how to allocate the dollars. She put half into company stock and half into a stock fund.

Teetering Tina now held a lot of Prime stock, both in her 401(k) and her stock options. Ten years of working for the firm and watching it grow made her confident that she had nothing to worry about.

Professional Perspective

There is no cast-in-concrete definition of a well-balanced portfolio. However, it's well worth figuring out the right balance for you. Portfolios are just like people—when they are off balance, they tend to fall. Tina didn't know that she should sell some of her shares of Prime and put some of the profit into other sectors. She didn't understand that she was leaving her portfolio overexposed to a potential earnings disaster by holding so much of one stock.

There are different ways of developing a balanced portfolio. Some of the variables that need to be considered are **risk tolerance, age of the portfolio owner, timeframe of needing access to money, overall goal for the portfolio,** and **general market conditions.** For the set-it-and-forget-it investor, there are lifestyle (or target) funds. These funds are developed based on specific criteria, such as a projected retirement date or a risk tolerance (conservative, moderate, or aggressive). Within these parameters there are different distribution targets, such 75% stocks, 20% bonds, and 5% cash. The fund manager keeps the fund invested and balanced to help maintain that objective.

A financial advisor works to develop a balanced portfolio for you that will be more personalized. Most likely your advisor will begin the process with a series of questions so that he or she can determine your investment objective (income vs. capital appreciation), your risk tolerance, and your goals for the money (such as retirement, a down payment on a home, or college planning).

A primary objective in developing a well-balanced portfolio is to achieve diversification among different types of investments—stocks, bonds, cash, domestic, international, etc. A diversified portfolio is so important because it is designed to help reduce the risk of the portfolio as a whole. Different investment types tend to move in different directions. Thus, when returns in the stock market are low, the bond market may be performing well. Over time, a well-diversified portfolio can provide higher returns than a portfolio too highly concentrated in one area. But there are no guarantees of better performance and it may not protect against loss in declining markets.

In our example above, Tina was fortunate enough to have accumulated a large amount of a well performing stock and enjoyed watching the value of this investment grow. It is now time to sell a portion of her position in this stock and bring the value of this investment category back down to the targeted amount. There are also certain circumstances that should trigger a rebalancing of a portfolio. They might be world conditions—inflation, the price of gas, war, etc.—or they might be personal life changing events—the death of a spouse, an impending major expenditure.

A portfolio is a constantly changing thing. It can't be developed and then put on the shelf, never to be looked at again. Whether you are managing it yourself or using a financial advisor, it needs to be reviewed at least annually.

Investment Planning—Quick Recap

Self-Analysis

- Everyone has a different investment personality type and a different comfort zone when it comes to how much they want to be involved in their investments.

- People today, however, are forced into taking a more active role in investing than were previous generations.

- The glut of information on the Internet can lead to paralysis.

- But there is no final piece of the puzzle. At some point, doing nothing is worse than making an imperfect decision. No one has a crystal ball, anyway—no decision will be perfect.

Picking Stocks

- Unlike with other kinds of purchases, last year's performance is often a poor indicator of how an investment will perform once you buy it.

- A financial advisor is trained to interpret all the data available and therefore may increase an investor's chances of better performance as well as reducing the investor's stress level.

- Water cooler wisdom rarely leads to much wealth. Discipline and balance is a better recipe for success.

Picking Mutual Funds

- Mutual funds with the same investment objectives often draw on the same universe of companies—so buying five different funds does *not* necessarily mean you have a diversified portfolio unless you've specifically compared the contents of those funds, or unless the funds have different objectives.

The Thrill of the Hunt

- If you need the thrill of playing the game, then keep a "mad money" fund that doesn't affect how much money you put away for your long-term goals.

- Remember the less-than-thrilling, but still essential, principles of long term investing: dollar cost averaging; reinvest your dividends, interest, and capital gains; pay attention to mutual fund fees and stock trading commissions as well as performance.

How Much Risk Can You Take?

- Bonds carry several kinds of risk, too.

- Young, volatile companies without a proven track record can result in high returns, but at great risk.

- You need to be able to honestly assess how much risk you can handle emotionally.

- One way to spread out the risk is to divide your investments into long-term and short-term objectives. You may be able to handle more risk in the long-term investments given that over the long term the market tends to go up.

- A financial advisor can help you determine your risk tolerance.

What to Buy, When to Sell

- It's essential to put emotion aside and buy and sell based on intellect and strict discipline.

- Doing nothing about your investment is a decision—it has consequences.

Balance

- A well-balanced portfolio achieves diversification among different types of investments—stocks, bonds, cash, domestic, international, etc.—thereby reducing the risk of the portfolio as a whole.

- A financial advisor can help achieve a balance that's more personalized.

- When circumstances change, your portfolio may need to be rebalanced. You should review your portfolio (on your own or with your advisor) at least annually.

RISK MANAGEMENT

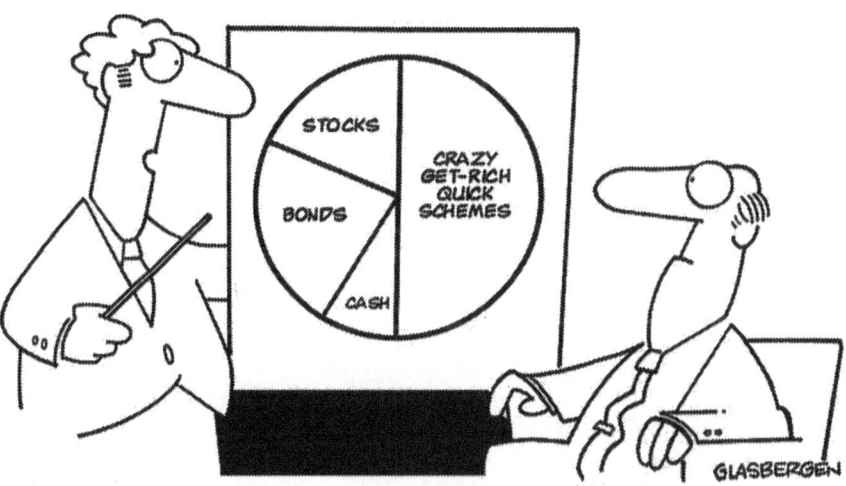

"I'd like you to consider a bold new strategy..."

Rainy Day Care

"Money can't buy you happiness but it does bring you a
more pleasant form of misery."

-Spike Milligan-

Robin worked at a radio station where sixty-hour workweeks were the norm. She loved what she did and she was good at it, but the lack of free time was starting to wear on her. Her husband, Gary, was used to her schedule—perhaps because he worked as many hours as she did.

When Robin found out she was pregnant, she and Gary had the first of many conversations about how they wanted to raise their children. Stay-at-home mom, stay-at-home-dad, nanny, daycare, some combination of all of the above—many imperfect options, each with its own set of pros and cons. Robin's career was important to her; on the other hand, the couple could manage on Gary's income alone, and not on hers.

One day, Robin found out she had two last-minute meetings and a changed deadline for a major project. The dishwasher repair guy was coming between three and five-thirty, she hadn't bought her mother a birthday present yet (although the party was scheduled for tomorrow), none of her clothes actually fit her any longer, and she had no time to do anything about any of it.

On that day, Robin realized that there was no way she was going to be able to do all this as well as raise a child the way she and Gary wanted to. When the two of them sat down later that evening, they made a decision. She was going to be a stay-at-home mom for a while.

Five years flew by. They had a second child and Robin's days were filled with taking care of the two children. She juggled their schedules, nap times, car pools, ballet lessons, play dates, ear infections, and so on, and so on. Gary continued to work the long hours, but they'd found a rhythm that seemed to work, for the time being.

And then the horror story you think could never happen to you and your family happened to Robin. One rainy Spring day, after Robin had dropped the kids off at friends' houses for play dates, an SUV ran a red light and slammed into the driver's side of her sedan. She was killed instantly.

The event shattered the lives of this family in every obvious way. But there were unforeseen financial consequences, too. Life goes on, in spite of everything; people go back to work, children need to be fed and taken places and cared for. Gary knew he had to get help in taking care of the two children while he worked the long hours his job required. He had a substantial life insurance policy on himself, but once Robin had stopped working, they hadn't kept up her policy. They'd felt that since she was no longer earning a salary, there was no need for insurance to replace her income—they could put the premiums towards paying other bills. He was beginning to realize what a mistake this had been.

By the time Gary added up the cost of pre-school, a nanny to pick the children up when they were done and watch them in the afternoon, a safe car for the nanny to drive his kids around in, someone for back-up on the mornings that one of the kids was sick and needed to stay home—or be brought to the doctor—he was overwhelmed. The two kids were having a hard enough time dealing with the loss of their mom. He didn't want to completely disrupt their normal routines, but he didn't know if he could afford to pay people to do what Robin had always done—at least, not without working another twenty hours a week. And he was barely keeping it together as it was.

Professional Perspective

Ah, life insurance. In its most basic form, the purpose of life insurance is to provide financial security. Insurance coverage pays out a specific amount of money to the beneficiaries upon the death of the insured. There are different types of life insurance, each with its own characteristics, uses, and benefits. For the scope of this book, the more complicated types of life insurance used for business or estate-planning purposes won't be covered.

The simplest use of life insurance is to provide money for your family if you should pass away. I'm always cautious about engaging a client who says his or her family is a top priority but who doesn't want to provide for them in the event of an untimely death. Life insurance is a necessary evil. It only pays off at the time of our demise, which is not something we actively want to consider. Traditionally, the breadwinner of the family is most concerned about coverage. But a stay-at-home parent needs coverage as well, because the surviving parent will need the additional resources to hire household help and pay for childcare. With a life insurance policy in place, both parents can rest somewhat assured that their family will be able to afford the help it needs should tragedy strike.

If life insurance makes sense for you, the next step is to determine how much coverage you require. These are some of the considerations to take into account:

- How much income will your family need for a transitional period until your spouse is ready to go back to work?

- Do you want your spouse to be able to pay off the mortgage?

- Do you want to have your children's college education paid for?

- Are you planning on the proceeds paying your funeral expenses?

- Other than your mortgage, how much debt do you have?

There are two basic types of life insurance: term insurance and permanent insurance (whole life, universal life). For most people, term insurance is the simplest and most cost effective.

Term insurance is a policy that lasts for a defined length of time (generally 5, 10, 20, or 30 years). You pay a premium each year for coverage and there is no built up cash value. The younger you are, the less expensive the premium. The policy is usually renewable without a medical examination. With annual renewable term, the premium will go up each time the policy is renewed because it is age-dependent. Level premium term insurance is just that—level throughout the term of the policy (the premium will be higher initially than annual renewable term but lower in the later years of the term).

Whole Life or Universal Life—cash value insurance—is a permanent policy (as opposed to a specified term). You are guaranteed coverage for life as long as you keep the premiums current. Some of each premium pays the administrative costs of the policy and the costs of the death benefit while the rest is invested. This invested portion becomes the cash value of the policy. The premiums for whole life insurance will be higher than term.

Deciding what type of insurance to buy, as well as how much coverage you need, can be complicated, but the decision may be critically important to the security of your family. A financial advisor will be able to review your needs, explain the various options available to you, and provide you with quotes for various levels of coverage. There may come a point in time when you no longer need to keep your life insurance because you are at a different stage of life. Here, too, your financial advisor can help you determine the most sensible thing to do.

Long Term Care, Short Term Decision

"Poverty is not a disgrace, but it's terribly inconvenient."

-Milton Berle-

Cracks in the Nest Egg

Jane and Michael were in their early seventies. Although they were senior citizens, they were still very active. They were living in a retirement village in Florida (where else!) where they had their own apartment and were able to participate freely in community activities such as bingo, golf, and backgammon. Michael was a retired plant manager, while Jane had stayed home to raise their three children.

Over the years, Michael and Jane had built quite a nice nest egg of about $400,000 for themselves. They had planned out exactly how much they would need to be able to pay their daily living expenses, as well as splurge every once in a while on vacation, or a celebratory dinner for their anniversary, or some other special occasion. While their retirement savings didn't allow them to live like royalty, it did afford them a comfortable lifestyle, similar to the way they lived during Michael's working years.

One morning Jane went down to the community pool where she went every morning to do her laps. She expertly fitted her swim cap over her hair after placing her towel on one of the nearby chairs. She slipped off her short terrycloth robe and thong flip flops, leaving them with her towel. At the shallow end of the pool, she slowly and carefully made her descent, grabbing the handrail and placing one foot at a time on the steps that led down into the water. As Jane was about to move down to the third and final step, she lost her balance, falling hard to the side. Her left hip struck the second step of the pool. The splash sounded like any other, but the pain Jane felt confirmed that she had broken something.

One ambulance ride later it was determined that Jane had severely shattered her hip and would need hip replacement surgery. The doctor explained to Michael that Jane would need extensive physical therapy and 24-hour care that Michael probably wouldn't be able to provide for her on his own. He suggested Michael look into a local nursing home that would give Jane round-the-clock care and attention. Michael knew the doctor was right and that he didn't have the ability to take care of Jane all by himself. Their children were all grown with families of their own, so he couldn't burden them with having to take care of him and Jane as well as their own needs.

After visiting the nursing home and meeting with the manager to go over the cost of having Jane live there, Michael's head was spinning. The fees for the nursing home came out to $3,000 per month. Adding this to current living expenses, Michael quickly figured out that their nice little retirement nest egg would soon dwindle down to nothing. How could such a short-term accident cause such long-term trauma?

Bread on Both Sides

It was a rainy Saturday afternoon in January, unusual for that time of year in South Florida. Gloria and Ron had just combed through the newspaper trying to decide what movie to see that evening. Ron wanted to catch the much-anticipated sequel to *The Matrix* while Gloria was leaning toward the remake of *The Stepford Wives.*

Suddenly the phone rang. Gloria answered with a gut feeling that something was terribly wrong.

Mrs. Richardson, her mom's next-door neighbor, spoke calmly but her voice was layered with concern. "Gloria, I think you need to come see your mom as soon as possible. Something's not quite right." When Gloria asked what Mrs. Richardson was implying, she said, "When I returned from the market and was unloading my groceries, I saw your mom in her front yard watering the flowers in her birthday suit!"

One week and three doctors later, it was clear that Gloria's mom was showing signs of Alzheimer's disease.

When Gloria's dad passed away four years earlier, she knew that her 68-year-old mom, Selma, would become her responsibility. A retired librarian, Selma was basically living off Social Security and a small pension that her husband left behind. It had never crossed her mind that one day she might not be in the position to take care of herself, physically or financially.

Meanwhile, Gloria's younger sister, Sheryl, was in no financial position to take care of her mom. She was going through a divorce and was too busy licking her own wounds. Also, living 1500 miles away in New Jersey, she was hardly a source of day-to-day emotional support for Gloria and Ron.

Raising two daughters in their impressionable teenage years was more than enough challenge for Gloria. The hormones were raging in her eldest daughter Cara, a junior in high school, while Michelle, a 13-year-old going on 30, could make your head spin with her daily, sometimes hourly, mood swings. Just a few days before, in an effort to communicate on neutral ground, Gloria asked Michelle, "How are things going with Jaden?" Jaden was the boy Michelle had a crush on. Michelle gave her mom a withering look and said, "You don't ever listen to me, Mom. His name is Jalen. And anyway, he is *so* lame! I'm going out with Tyler now." And Gloria thought she was on top of things!

Gloria and Ron were considered well off financially. They had diligently saved for college for both girls and had a sizeable nest egg for retirement.

At 48 and 50 years old respectively, Gloria and Ron were in their prime earning years and on top of the world. Ron had just made partner at a successful mid-size architectural firm. Gloria had been doing social work for the city ever since re-entering the job market after the girls reached elementary school age.

The thought of caring for Selma on a day-to-day basis was overwhelming. Despite Gloria's love for her mother, the financial burden was a lot to bear. How would she manage to be there for her mom during regular work hours? Would she need to cut back to part-time?

The feeling was so powerful that Gloria made a promise to herself never to put Cara and Michelle in that position.

Gloria and Ron came to see me the following Monday to discuss their need for Long-Term Care (LTC) insurance.

Professional Perspective

Gloria and Ron's predicament is not as uncommon as one might think. It is often referred to as the problem of the "the sandwich generation," a middle-aged couple with both their kids and parents dependent upon them.

Jane and Michael had lived carefully and built a secure future that in one split second was in jeopardy. Few of us can pay nursing home bills out-of-pocket for any extended period of time.

In their case, Gloria and Ron were jolted by the abruptness of their life change. It's impossible to predict when someone's health may take a turn for the worse.

There isn't an exact age or time to consider Long-Term Care (LTC) insurance. Many factors need to be considered before you can make a prudent decision. The key is that you need to start the decision-making process. Most parents don't want to end up as a burden to their children. Although some children don't want their parents to spend their inheritance, most children don't want to see their parents in a less than ideal facility. Waiting until you are actually faced with the situation means you will have fewer options available.

It is clear that Selma would have benefited from having LTC insurance in place. Whether it was in the form of home care or nursing home care, Gloria would have had assistance in taking care of her mom. In addition to caring for her mom's physical well being, Gloria now finds herself responsible for her mom's finances.

In the United States, the type of care you are entitled to is a direct function of your ability to pay for it. If you do not have the resources, you still are entitled to care, but it may not be of the quality you would desire. Depending on personal assets, you may qualify for Medicaid benefits, which could ease the burden on the supporting family. It is critical to speak with your financial advisor or an elder care attorney in the state in which you reside to determine current regulations and what benefits you may be entitled to.

Gloria and Ron, at age 48 and 50 respectively, are on the younger side to be considering LTC insurance. As mentioned earlier, there is no right time to purchase this form of insurance, but there are certainly times when it is too soon or too late.

As with almost all forms of insurance (e.g. life, disability, auto, and home), we purchase insurance to hedge against the risk of loss. With automobiles, insurance is a method of protecting us from incurring a financially devastating expense due to an accident that results in damage to the vehicle, passenger, bystanders, or other property. In the case of life insurance, we are using insurance to replace income, cover a debt, or help pay for future family goals that were important to us in our lifetime. Without the insurance, our family could be left destitute.

LTC insurance is no different. We purchase insurance to minimize out-of-pocket expenses in the event we can no longer care for ourselves. Many times, the care of one spouse can deplete a couple's entire retirement savings. Upon the demise of that spouse, the survivor is left with little or no means of providing for his or her own needs.

It makes the most sense to purchase LTC insurance when the risk of illnesses increases, but before it is too great. The recommended age range is 45 to 70. Earlier than 45, you'll likely find yourself paying premiums for many years before you need to (a breakeven analysis should be performed by your financial advisor). Later than 70, and you run the risk of not qualifying for insurance due to possible pre-existing health conditions.

Family history is a consideration. Gloria's dad passed away in his early sixties. Her mom, Selma, was diagnosed with Alzheimer's at age 68. Gloria is a prime candidate for LTC insurance prior to the age of 60. Her premiums may be higher than others because she is more likely to need the benefits of her policy.

Financially, Gloria and Ron can afford the premiums of an LTC policy, which may range from $1,000 per year per person, to $5,000 or more, depending on health, age, and benefits desired.

If you are of particularly robust financial means, it may not be necessary for you to have LTC insurance since you can, in essence, self-insure. This means that you can afford to pay for your care out-of-pocket. Your sufficient nest egg would not only take care of any LTC expenses, but would still leave a necessary amount of money to care for the surviving or healthy spouse.

Some people find themselves in the opposite situation. They may be of limited financial means and the cost of LTC insurance premiums would tap them out or come at the expense of another necessity. This, of course, is a personal decision. Regardless, the decision whether or not to purchase LTC insurance should be considered carefully well before the benefits are likely to be needed.

To summarize, consider the following when evaluating the need for LTC insurance:

- Age—usually purchased between the ages of 45 and 70
- Family health and longevity history
- Financial means—ability to pay the premiums or the care itself
- Type of care—private home care or nursing home care (or both)

Health Insurance Makes Me Sick

"Money is good for bribing yourself through the inconveniences of life."

-Gottfried Reinhardt-

Simon was considering shutting the doors to the business after 37 years of operation. His pride and joy had run its course and had been barely profitable the past two years.

His mom-and-pop pharmacy could no longer compete with the big chains. It seemed like a new CVS or Walgreens was popping up every other day, not to mention the competition from every Publix pharmacy and Super Wal-Mart.

Lisa, his wife, had stood by his side during the good times, great times, and the ugly years. Although he would never admit it, Lisa was the backbone of the company. Simon handled day-to-day operations, but the key decisions were passed through Lisa. She had a great business sense and a wonderful rapport with the customers. Lisa would always say "Simon has the pharmaceutical degree, but...."

The pressure of the business had gotten to Simon. Looking at his college yearbook picture was torture. He had gained nearly 45 pounds and who knows how much body fat since college and it had taken its toll on him.

When Simon was diagnosed with type 2 diabetes three years ago, he vowed to make fitness and diet a priority in his life. He and his son Michael would leave it all out on the tennis court every Monday and Thursday night. In fact, every once in a while he was still able to take a set from Michael.

Simon used to dream about the day Michael would take over the business. What a proud moment for a father and such a graceful way to transition into retirement.

Michael, however, had other plans. His law degree from the University of Florida landed him a job at a prestigious law firm in Boca Raton. Unbeknownst to his father, the thought of running the pharmacy had never held any appeal for him. He knew all along he was never going to take the reins, but he didn't have the heart to ever tell his dad.

As Lisa was thinking about the odds and ends of closing the pharmacy, it dawned on her that they had been running the health insurance through the shop all these years. With the business closing and with Simon's diabetes, how would they qualify for affordable health insurance?

Simon, while eligible for Social Security now that he had turned 62, was three years away from qualifying for Medicare. They weren't familiar with the rules of COBRA (Consolidated Omnibus Budget Reconciliation Act) and they couldn't fathom bearing the cost of health care expenses alone.

When Simon and Lisa came to the conclusion that they needed help, they thought they were prepared for the worst.

Professional Perspective

This is one of the more difficult situations that face the self-employed and business owners today, and not just when facing retirement.

Providing health insurance for employees has become one of the costliest parts of running a small business. The employees need and deserve a benefit package, and the owners, in order to retain these employees, must provide it.

Simon and Lisa have been hit with the double whammy. They desperately need the health insurance. Simon knows first hand the cost of medicine. Simon's monthly insulin and needle supply alone runs to $500, and that doesn't take into account the test strips and lancets for his glucometer, or his quarterly visits to the endocrinologist.

All totaled, Simon's health upkeep would run them nearly $2,000 per month without any surprises or other ailments.

Lisa had done her research before they came to see us. She shopped around on the Internet for health plans but to no avail. She also found out that COBRA would only last for 18 months after they closed the shop. She was totally dejected and desperate for a solution.

There weren't very many options for Simon and Lisa. The two plausible solutions that came to mind were:

1.   Keep the shop open for another few years and continue running the health insurance through the business.

They would need the pharmacy just to break even (after modest salaries) for another two years. Simon would have to swallow his pride as the business continued to tailspin.

After the two years, they could then use COBRA for 18 months until Simon qualified for Medicare. At that point, Lisa could apply for health insurance as an individual. Being in good health, it appeared that this would not be much of a problem. However, she would be taking the risk of developing a condition in that period of time that might prohibit her from being eligible for health insurance.

2   Lisa and/or Simon could get part-time or full-time employment with another firm that provided health benefits. (Upon early retirement, one of my clients—a big-time corporate executive—took a part-time job at the local outlet of a clothing chain. With health benefits and a friendly, easy-going work environment, it was an easy way to manage health care costs for a few years.)

With their solid résumés, Lisa and Simon both should have been able to find work with any one of their competitors. Once Simon got past his pride, he would realize this was the path of least resistance. He could easily squeak out a decent salary for reduced hours, and be eligible for health benefits.

This may be a good opportunity to discuss COBRA. There are many scenarios in addition to Lisa and Simon's where understanding COBRA becomes important in making a good decision. Passed in 1986, it gives certain groups of people the right to continue group health insurance. Examples of those groups of people include former employees, former spouses, and dependant children. The participant usually has to pay the premium himself or herself, but it is usually less expensive than having to pay for individual coverage. Certain qualifying events, such as divorce or employment termination, must occur for eligibility. COBRA coverage can last from 18 to 36 months depending upon the qualifying event.

Health insurance and the cost of prescription medication is an area of hot debate. Too often, those who need insurance the most can't afford it, and those who are a picture of health have access to its benefits. The system is awfully screwy. If I could provide a reasonable solution in this book I would. But then I'd probably be too busy running for office, maybe even for President of the United States. Not that having *that* job does any wonders for your health.

When You're Hurt and Can't Work

"Rich or poor, what one needs is enough money."

-Welsh proverb-

The residents of Middleton were used to seeing Jason riding his bike. A teacher at the local private high school, he was well known and well liked by everyone. He was always active and kept himself physically fit. Recently he had been taking his bike riding more seriously and had begun to train for some amateur competitions.

Jason usually went out to train late in the afternoon after all his school related activities were done. With a one-and a three-year-old, he knew that once he got home, he'd never get back out to train. He and Jennifer married right out of college and were happy with the routines and life they had established.

That Friday afternoon he didn't go out to train. A group of teachers from the high school were going out to a Country & Western bar to celebrate a birthday. After a few drinks, Jason decided to try the mechanical bull. Why, not? He was in great shape and how hard could it be?

The first few rounds were easy. With his friends urging him on, he decided to try a harder ride. Holding on for dear life, he felt like his body was being tossed around like a rag doll. Instead of calling out to tell them to stop the bull, his competitive spirit told him that he could last another minute. Oh boy, if he could only take that last minute back.

Life changed for Jason in a few seconds. He went flying off the bull with his arms and legs flailing in all directions. He had a number of badly broken bones and some internal injuries. Nothing was life threatening but it was obvious that he had a very long road to recovery ahead of him.

Jason was spending hours each day at rehab and when he got home he was exhausted and depressed. Jennifer was stretched to the limit trying to take care of the kids and the house, figure out how she was going to get a part-time job, and remain understanding of Jason's emotional state. The families at the high school were wonderful and had put together a fundraiser. That was helping for right now but wouldn't last for long.

Jason had medical insurance and some sick time accumulated, but being young and with a young family he didn't have much in the way of savings. Jennifer hadn't worked since their children were born and neither of them came from families that were able to help them out financially. Now not only was Jason facing the stress of a long rehabilitation, he was even more stressed about how he was going to take care of his family.

Professional Perspective

While most of us don't go around riding mechanical bulls, we all know that accidents and illnesses happen. Disabilities often bring high medical costs as well as costs associated with accommodating your disability, not to mention the potential loss of your capacity to work and take care of your family. All of which is to state the obvious: accidents can have devastating financial consequences. Some people have disability insurance through their employer, but few of us think about taking out a private policy.

There are several things to look for in a disability insurance policy. Probably one the more important items to look for is coverage for "owner's occupation" vs. "any occupation." **Owner's occupation** means that you are covered if you can't work at your current occupation. **Any occupation** coverage will only kick in if you can't work at any occupation at all.

Ideally, you would like your policy to have residual benefits. This means that you will be guaranteed a certain percentage of the income you made in the job you no longer can perform. For example, assume you have owner's occupation coverage with a 75% residual benefit. In your old job you made $80,000 and in the new job you are only making $50,000. Your policy will pay you $10,000 per year (75% of $80,000 is $60,000 and you are only making $50,000).

Another item to look for is cost-of-living adjustments. Without this kind of a rider, your coverage will not keep up with inflation. As we all experience every day at the grocery store and gas station, the $1,000 per month that seemed like plenty of money five years ago won't get you nearly as far today.

You should consider a disability policy even if you have worker's compensation. Worker's compensation is only applicable if you are injured at work. A disability policy covers you regardless of where or how you became injured or ill.

There are times when we all feel like we are on insurance overload. By the time we think about health insurance, life insurance, property insurance, car insurance, and—depending on where we live—flood and wind insurance, about the last thing we want to do is research more insurance. But the reality is, if you are hurt and can't work (this sounds like the duck on that commercial talking) either temporarily or permanently, your family's security may be jeopardized.

For the Organizationally Challenged

"Always remember, money isn't everything—but also
remember to make a lot of it before talking
such fool nonsense."

-Earl Wilson-

Helen had worked in the finance industry for years. Now fifty, she decided she wanted to learn to play bridge. Her mother had been playing bridge forever and Helen knew it was a great way to meet new people in any type of social arena. She did some research to discover where there were beginners courses offered and found one that suited her schedule.

Living in South Florida, she found that most people in the class were considerably older than she was. She and the other three middle age women started to play together each week in class. After a few weeks, they decided it would be nice to meet for dinner beforehand.

They had a pleasant dinner and conversation. When it was time to pay the bill and get to class, three of them took wallets out to get their money. Lily thrust her hand into her pocketbook and pulled out a fist full of wadded up cash. Everyone looked at this mess of bills, different denominations all crunched up into a ball, and raised their eyebrows questioningly. Not the least bit embarrassed, Lily said she wasn't very organized and she just shoved her cash into her pocketbook. Sometimes when she didn't feel like figuring out how much money she had, she just went to the bank and got more!

After a few more lessons they decided it was time to play bridge outside of class to practice what they were learning. Lily offered to host the group the following Saturday afternoon. After class, while walking to the cars in the parking lot, Lily took Helen aside and asked if she might be able to come over a little earlier as she had some things she wanted to ask her about.

Helen got to Lily's house a half hour early, not sure what Lily wanted to talk to her about. After chatting for a few minutes, Lily took Helen into the room she used as her office. Helen gasped as she looked around the room—there were papers stacked everywhere. Lily was a successful social worker but it was obvious that organization wasn't in her skill set. Lily asked Helen if she would be willing to come over and help her go through the papers, set up her files, tell her what she could shred, and let her know if she was missing any important documents. She was willing to pay her to do this. Helen said she would and they set up their first appointment for one night the following week.

Helen arrived, wearing jeans and a t-shirt, ready to tackle the project. Sitting on the floor, file folders and labels beside her, she started on the first stack. She nearly began to hyperventilate as she found current bills in the same pile as brokerage statements from 1995, a living will mixed in with recipes for a low-fat diet, and a medical proxy that had never been completed stuck to old receipts from Nordstrom. This was definitely more than a one-day project.

Professional Perspective

Organizing important documents and maintaining that organization is a challenge for all of us. Somehow, getting papers into piles by category, shredding the old stuff, and figuring out how to keep the important stuff safe isn't how many of us want to spend our Saturday afternoon. But when a situation arises that requires us to get our hands on some document quickly, and we can't find it, we realize how critical the task is.

There are different methods for organizing our papers. Many of us keep things like the title to the car and the deed to the house in a safe deposit box. The idea is that even if the house burns down or floods, these papers will be safe. We also don't need ready access to these documents, so having them out of the house doesn't pose an inconvenience.

There are some accordion filing systems available that will help structure your papers by category. This is certainly better than having the papers stacked on the floor like Lily, but as anyone in a flood or hurricane zone can attest to, this is still not a great solution.

There are software programs available that will help you collect and store important information including the locations of important documents, account numbers, and contact names and addresses. This can be a good source of information for family members if you are incapacitated.

Our firm has a product, "The Vault," that combines many of these aspects of document management. We will scan our clients' important documents—such as living wills, trusts, contact data, etc.—into our computer and produce a CD-ROM for them. They will then have all their information in one place and we will also have it stored on our computer. That eliminates the risk of losing all their information in the event of a fire or flood.

One other important piece of the paper overload puzzle is **how long to keep documents.** The following are some rules of thumb. (You should ask your tax advisor any specific questions you may have regarding document retention.)

- Tax returns and supporting documentation should be kept for **seven years.**

- Bank statements should be kept for **three years.**

- Trading records showing what you paid for a stock/mutual fund should be kept **until the year after you sell the investment.**

- Home improvement receipts should be kept **until three years after the house is sold.**

Some of us find organization to be second nature. Some of us find the task deadly, and therefore don't do it. The important thing is to find the tools that are available to make the process as painless and as efficient as possible.

Risk Management—Quick Recap

Life Insurance

- Traditionally the breadwinner of the family is most concerned about life insurance coverage, but stay-at-home parents need coverage as well.

- Term insurance is a policy that lasts for a defined length of time, with no cash value buildup.

- Whole life (or cash value) insurance is a permanent policy guaranteeing coverage for life as long as the premiums are current. A portion of the premium is invested and becomes the cash value of the policy.

Long-Term Care Insurance

- Few of us can pay nursing home bills out-of-pocket for any extended period of time. LTC can minimize those expenses in the event that we can no longer care for ourselves.

- The recommended age range for purchasing LTC is 45 – 70, but family health history and financial means should be taken into account.

- You can purchase LTC for private home care or nursing home care (or both).

Health Insurance for the Self-Employed and Small Business Owners

- You really need to think ahead to make sure you have a way to cover yourself between retirement (or selling your business) and the time Medicare kicks in.

- Ask your financial advisor about COBRA and what it can and can't do for you.

Disability Insurance

- Worker's compensation is only applicable if you are injured at work. Disability insurance covers you for loss of income regardless of where or how you are injured.

- Owner's occupation insurance covers you if you can't work at your current occupation

- Any-occupation coverage only kicks in if you can't work at any occupation at all.

Organizing Your Information

- It's a thankless task, but it's important to have all your vital documents in order and accessible should you need them in an emergency.

- One way to do this is to scan the documents and keep CD-ROMs in several locations.

RETIREMENT PLANNING

© 2003 Randy Glasbergen.

"Explain to me one more time why enjoying life when
I retire is more important than enjoying life now."

Anti-Social Security

"Retirement at sixty-five is ridiculous. When I was sixty-five I still had pimples."

-George Burns-

Vicki and Al were street smart and considered themselves pros when it came to taking advantage of the system. They compared dozens of cell phone plans to get the most minutes for their money. They scrutinized credit card offers to get the best cash-back awards and frequent flier miles. They timed their trips to Costco to coincide with lunch or dinner so they could dine on free food samples. (You know who you are.) Now approaching 62, Al was faced with deciding whether or not to start collecting Social Security.

As with all his other decisions, Al decided he wanted to figure out all the angles. The big question was whether to collect the lower monthly benefits now, or wait until he reached 66 or 70 to collect more money. He didn't talk about it with Vicki, but his health wasn't the best. Vicki knew this, but she didn't want to dwell on the subject since it upset both of them.

According to his Social Security statement, if Al waited to collect until he was 70, he'd receive about $700 more per month than if he started to collect at 66 (about $1,250 more than at age 62). He figured that was a better deal. After all, the additional benefit would cover a big piece of the monthly lease payments on their cars at that time. Vicki wasn't great at math so she went along with Al's decision to wait until age 70 to begin collecting Social Security.

Several years went by and those years weren't the best for Vicki and Al. Al had health issues that were getting worse, not better. He'd switched all his credit cards to cash-back rewards and not frequent flier miles, since he and Vicki didn't feel up to traveling. Their Costco sampling days were done and now they were looking more for the early bird specials at the local deli. They'd even begun thinking about giving up one car, as there were many days Al didn't feel well enough to drive.

All of Vicki and Al's dealings with us had been over the phone for the past year so when they walked into our office I was surprised to see how Al looked. That brash, confident guy was gone. They were here to go over their income needs now that Al's health issues had driven up their expenses. The first thing we talked about was the fact that Al hadn't been collecting his Social Security for the past two years, which amounted to close to $40,000 in lost income.

Professional Perspective

Almost all retirees are faced with a decision when they become eligible for Social Security retirement benefits. Throughout their working career, each individual receives an annual statement of estimated benefits from Social Security approximately 3 months prior to his or her birthday. This statement projects Social Security benefits that the retiree is entitled to upon reaching the age of 62, 66, and 70. The monthly benefits get progressively larger as you delay taking them.

For instance, a 52-year-old who earns $100,000 per year consistently and who has contributed to the system for the past 20 years could be entitled to the following (see www.irs.gov):

Age 62: $1,614 per month
Age 66: $2,167 per month
Age 70: $2,881 per month

How do you decide when to claim your benefit?

The factors involved include **life expectancy**, **income need**, and **projected return on investment**. As with any decision involving multiple variables, it's difficult to weigh all the pieces.

Let's try to address each variable separately. If you are experiencing health issues, it may not be in your best interests to postpone collecting your benefits. Even if your health is fine, examining your family health history may be unpleasant but a necessary task. If you aren't in good health, then it seems impractical to forego $1,614 per month for a number of years in order to try to collect $1,267 more per month (that's $2,881–$1,614) by waiting until you're 70.

As an aside, when a spouse passes away, if the deceased spouse's Social Security income was greater, the surviving spouse will begin to receive the greater amount. The surviving spouse no longer collects his or her own amount.

Another variable to address is what other sources of income you have. How much income do you require each month and how much income are your investments generating for you? If your investments aren't providing you with enough income, the decision is simple—you need the Social Security income to make ends meet.

Here's another potential piece to the puzzle. Suppose you start to collect your Social Security as soon as you're eligible, and your concern is that you will be getting a lesser monthly benefit. You fear you'll need to withdraw more income from your investments in order to have enough cash each month—in the example earlier in this discussion, the difference between waiting and receiving benefits right away was $1,267 per month. If you are in good health, another solution may be working part-time in order to make up this $1,267 each month. You'd get the additional income you need without having to take more income out of your investments. This way you could reinvest all of your interest and dividends to take advantage of compounding. You might end up with significantly more investment income at 70 than the $1,267 more per month you would have received from Social Security for waiting.

As with many financial decisions, a tax or legal professional will be able to assist you in weighing all of your options. He or she will be able to analyze your own specific circumstances and any potential tax consequences. This type of quantitative and qualitative analysis may make the final decision a little more clear.

Jackpot Judy

"Luck? I don't know anything about luck. I've never banked on it and I'm afraid of people who do. Luck to me is something else: Hard work—and realizing what is opportunity and what isn't."

-Lucille Ball-

After inheriting over $400,000, a 56-year-old middle school librarian was referred to our firm by another broker. She walked into our offices on a cool Monday morning with large clunky shoes, tight curly brown hair, and a shy demeanor. The getting-to-know-you conversation was limited by her mono-tone, one-word replies. Otherwise, the meeting seemed fairly straightforward.

Our premise was to make her money last her through retirement, so we advised her to withdraw a specific amount from her account each month calculated to reasonably predict that the inheritance lasted. Sipping her green tea, she appeared pleased with our proposal. She smiled nervously, shook our hands, and walked out the door.

For a couple of months, everything was serene.

When month three came around, we began receiving peculiar phone calls from her saying she needed more money. Per her request we made sure the funds were available.

For the next four months, the phone calls continued. These calls always seemed to come when she was traveling out of town.

We realized there was more to the story when she began calling to ask where her money was going. It was obvious to us she was taking out more money than what we'd agreed upon and her account was quickly disintegrating.

After a little bit of research, we soon discovered her little secret. She was taking frequent trips to Vegas!

Neither my partner nor I suspected her hidden hobby; we took her for a scrab-ble player at best but hardly a gambler. Looking back, I suppose we should have had some sort of a clue—her email address read "jackpot_ judy@...."

She eventually left the firm claiming we didn't manage her funds well enough. I'm not sure what kind of management she was looking for, but she was right about this much: neither my partner nor I are any good at blackjack.

Professional Perspective

Social Security, pensions, investments, and inheritances are all part of an over-all retirement plan that will take a different form for each individual. Not only does each person draw on a different combination of income sources, but each person also has a distinct financial personality to take into account.

The first step in developing a retirement plan is to determine what you want your lifestyle to be and how much income you will need each month to support that lifestyle. It is critical at this stage of the planning process to very honestly assess how you currently live. Probably most of us aren't Las Vegas high rollers at heart, but each of us has our own weaknesses when it comes to spending our money. Whether we want to eat all of our meals out, plan a major trip each year, or own the newest electronic gadgetry, addressing these issues is critical to developing a retirement plan that will work.

But our real spending habits are often a little different from what we think they are. In other words, we need data, not just impressions. People have their own methods for gathering this data, but the bills and monthly statements form the baseline. After that, you need to know how you're spending your everyday cash. Some people carry a little spiral notebook with them and jot down all their cash purchases. Some people charge all of their purchases whenever the option is available, which allows them to capture this data on their monthly statements. One of my clients kept the receipts for every purchase, no matter how small, and placed them in a Ziploc bag. Once a week they entered the information into a personal finance software program. It may take a few months of data collection to get a representative sample of information on which to base a plan.

This stage of planning leads us to do something we all enjoy about as much as going to the dentist—budgeting. As tedious as a budget may be to set up, the benefits to be gained from it in the long run are huge. It doesn't matter if your income is $30,000 per year or $300,000—you still have to plan how to allocate those dollars.

You need to sit down (with your spouse, if you're married) and hash out a spending plan. What's out, what's in, how much—the process can become quite emotional. Some couples can't do this without an independent third party walking them through it. People tend to get defensive about those items that are important to them that their partners don't understand. My suggestion is first to establish those expenses that are fixed—the mortgage, car payments, the utilities, insurance, gas, etc. Then see how much is left for the more variable types of expenses, such as clothing, recreation, dining out, or travel. The key here is to be realistic, fair, and willing to compromise. (Sounds like marriage in general!)

Before this budget is declared final, track actual vs. budget spending for a few months to ensure that the budget you've developed is realistic or that you haven't overlooked some important items. The purpose of a budget is to give you a road map for achieving your goals. It must be useable or it won't be of much value to you.

Once you've retired, the next critical step is implementing the income and spending plan you developed. Overspending and then constantly having to dip into principle means that there is a greater likelihood of outlasting your money. Even if things don't come to such a desperate pass, the fact is that the less money you've invested, the less income you receive, thus further increasing the likelihood of outliving your money or having to go back to work at age 80.

For those lucky enough to receive an inheritance, whether expected or a windfall, proper planning can make a dramatic difference. Develop a plan for the inherited money similar to your retirement money strategy instead of blowing it all in a short time period. This can be especially critical for the person who isn't experienced at handling large (and the definition of large is different for every person) lump sums of money. Everyone deserves a treat—denial isn't a good thing either—but before making any drastic spending decisions you need to have a logical plan in place.

Home, Home on the Market

"Money will buy you a bed, but not a good night's sleep,
a house but not a home, a companion but not a friend."

-Zig Ziglar

Bob and Sue bought their first house two weeks after their wedding. It wasn't what most people would have considered a dream house, but it had real potential. They were able to get the two-bedroom Key West style home for well below the market value because, as the broker pointed out, there were those little matters of a new roof, new windows, new floors, new doors, and a few other minor repairs to take care of. Ten years and $175,000 in improvements later, the house was perfect—the home of their dreams. They even built an additional wing with an extra bedroom and bathroom. They decided they would stay there, even after their twins left for college. Finally, they would have their dream house all to themselves!

Bob and Sue, now close to retirement, had invested their funds conservatively, but wisely (as you can see with the house). However, after a detailed evaluation of all their finances, they found that they might need to postpone retirement and the two week Alaskan cruise they had talked about for years. In fact, they might have to really scale down their lifestyle. There just wasn't enough in the coffers to compensate for the way prices were rising across the board.

They read the newspapers and listened to everyone talk about real estate values. When a home in the neighborhood sold, everyone chatted in amazement about how much it had gone for. Bob and Sue would sit at the kitchen table over a cup of coffee, comparing the features of their house to the house that sold and trying to guess how much their home might be worth. Never in a million years would they have thought they'd own something worth that amount of money.

Their twins came home for a visit and sensed something was up. Bob and Sue didn't like to worry their children about money problems but the twins pushed. Reluctantly, Sue explained the conflicted position they were in. They loved their house and had planned on living there forever. They lingered at the penciled-in height marks on the door frame in the kitchen, they laughed about the day the dog ran straight through the screen door to go after the neighbor's cat, and they groaned remembering some of the long days of working on fixer-upper projects. But with their nest egg and ability to save not enough to support the lifestyle they had anticipated, they felt that maybe they could no longer afford to stay there.

On the other hand, on paper they were richer than they felt because the value of the house had gone up by so much. But that didn't seem to be doing them much good on a day-to-day basis. Sue sighed, rested her head on Bob's shoulder, and told the twins that they just didn't know the right thing to do.

Professional Perspective

The enormous rise in property values in many parts of the country has resulted in a dilemma for many people. They have built up a tremendous amount of equity in their home but may need additional income for their retirement lifestyle. They are asset rich but feel cash poor.

Depending on the market conditions in the part of the country you live in, one option to consider is to sell your home and find something less expensive to live in. The excess cash from the transaction can then be invested to provide you with the additional income you need for retirement. A financial advisor will be able to give you an idea of how much money you may need to invest and suggest an investment strategy. This projection will be one factor in determining whether or not selling your home is the right answer for you. Of course, the emotional difficulty of parting with the house you've raised your family in may be great—this will differ for everyone.

Selling the house and downsizing to something smaller and less expensive is not the only option, or even necessarily the best one from a strictly financial standpoint. Once you start looking around and examining the numbers, you may find—again, depending on where you live—that this strategy won't actually save you as much money as you thought. While your home has appreciated, it's likely that everyone else's has, as well. You may find that you have to spend far more than you'd thought in order to find something you can tolerate living in.

Another issue is property taxes. Property taxes are calculated differently in each state—in Florida, for example, your property taxes can only go up by a certain percentage each year if you use your homestead exemption. But when the property is sold, the taxes are re-calculated based upon current assessed value. It's quite possible that property taxes on the newer, downsized house are higher than on your current house. For example, say you bought a house for

$300,000. Ten years later, the house is worth $600,000 but you are only paying $6,500 in property tax on it. You decide to downsize, sell your home, and buy a smaller place for $400,000. Your taxes might start at $8,000—that's $1,500 more than the property tax you were paying on a much larger and more valuable house.

There's another option: staying in your home and taking out a **reverse mortgage**. As the name suggests, a reverse mortgage is basically the opposite of a regular mortgage. You use the equity you've built up in your home to get income. You still own your home; the title is still in your name. You are also still responsible for all taxes and insurance on your home. Here are some of the basics of a reverse mortgage:

- You must be at least 62 years of age to qualify for a reverse mortgage.

- The amount you can borrow depends on your age, the value of your home, and current interest rates. You can receive income on a regular schedule, receive one lump sum, or establish a line of credit to use as needed.

- The loan gets repaid when the property is sold or when the owner passes away. If your heirs want to keep the house, they will have to repay the loan.

- There are costs incurred when taking out a reverse mortgage. As with a regular mortgage, the costs can be built into the amount of the reverse mortgage.

For people like Bob and Sue who would like to stay in their home, but are having income difficulties, a reverse mortgage may be the solution. They can take advantage of the equity they've built up over the years to help finance the retirement lifestyle they've been dreaming about. Before proceeding with a big step like this, Bob and Sue should see their financial advisor to make sure they understand the reverse mortgage, and costs associated, and to help them work out all the numbers involved.

Hypertension Pension

"Money is better than poverty, if only for financial reasons."

-Woody Allen-

Hard Landing

Howie and Sally arrived for their initial meeting with us seconds before it was scheduled to start. Energy and tension were just radiating off of Howie. We settled around the conference table and before I had a chance to start the meeting, I could see Howie jiggling his leg and tapping his pen. I was unsure what prompted them to meet with us, so I asked them to fill me in on why they were here. Howie took charge immediately and began to tell me his story.

Howie knew he wanted to be a pilot from the time he was thirteen years old. As a teenager he spent his free time researching the career path that would take him to a job with the commercial airlines. Whenever he got the chance, he went to the airport and spoke with the pilots to find out the steps to take along the way.

Howie met Sally when he was working for a small commuter airline. He wasn't making much money but he compared his situation with that of a doctor in training. He felt he was doing his internship now, paying his dues. The couple was confident that Howie would find his dream job with a major airline and earn the traditional benefits that went along with that type of employment.

Finally, when Howie was in his late twenties, he had accumulated enough experience to begin to interview with the major airlines. When the job offer came in, Howie and Sally threw a party for their friends and family to celebrate the achievement of his childhood dream. Secure in the knowledge that a dependable, steady income was waiting for them when Howie reached retirement, Howie and Sally lived comfortably but not extravagantly. They saved money to pay for their children's college education as well as to supplement their pension.

But the ground rules of retirement benefits were changing all around them—and fast. Upset and angry, the two of them knew that they had to do some serious financial planning. Howie had been in a physically stressful job his entire career. Would that have an impact on his life span? He wanted to make sure that Sally was well taken care of and didn't have to worry about her financial security after he was gone. By law, pilots must retire at age sixty, so they needed to plan their finances for a potentially long retirement. Howie had friends and coworkers who had already reached retirement age; he was aware of the pension decisions he was going to face. The couple realized that they simply didn't know how to factor in all the pieces of the puzzle, and their anxiety was mounting.

An Officer But Not a Gentleman

Mike also knew what he wanted to be from the time he was in his early teens. He graduated from high school and went straight to the Police Academy. He was a tough, opinionated guy and wasn't afraid to speak out. The other men in his class at the academy became his best friends. They worked together, trained together, partied together, and philosophized together.

Hanging out in the training rooms and offices at the Police Station was a lot like being in a locker room. The off-color jokes and magazines that circulated among the officers were just part of the atmosphere, and no one took offense at them. Mike, the ultimate macho guy, was always in the midst of the banter.

Sarah worked as a secretary in the Courthouse. She saw Mike around the building periodically, and whenever she did he always came over to chat with her. She thought he was a hunk. After several months of flirting, they started to date. Everyone thought they were a great looking couple. Mike loved being a policeman and was good at what he did. After a few years of dating and several promotions, Mike and Sarah got married.

Their friends gave them a hard time about how old-fashioned they were. Mike was definitely the "head of the household." Sarah quietly took care of the house and children. Mike's friends from the police force still made up his main social circle and they still spent a lot of off-duty time together. Sarah never wanted to rock the boat so she rarely complained.

One day a retirement and pension expert came in to the precinct to run a seminar on planning for retirement. He explained the benefit plans available and the repercussions of each. Given the high risk of their chosen profession, many of the officers were concerned about planning for their wives and children. Mike and his buddies laughingly commented that they wanted to be able to enjoy whatever retirement they had coming to them—after all, they'd earned it. They weren't going to take smaller monthly benefits and skimp just so their wives could enjoy life more after they died.

Professional Perspective

Prior to 1990, it was quite normal for an individual to work at a single company for his or her entire career (25-35 years), to retire with a pension, and be showered with gifts (remember the famous gold watch?). Today, employees of municipal, state, and federal governments still adhere to this approach (i.e. teachers, police, fire, postal, etc.), but few others do.

Today's employment landscape is largely empty of the loyalty corporations once had for their employees, and vice versa. In addition, the traditional defined benefit retirement (pension) plan that most corporations offered has been replaced with the much more well-known defined contribution plan (i.e. 401(k)). The corporation transferred the responsibility of funding the employee's retirement to the employee (a whole other topic for a possible *Not So Funny* sequel).

Getting back to the matter at hand, there is still a large population of baby boomers who fall into the pension plan retirement fund scenario. While corporate America may have converted to a 401(k) retirement plan, highly tenured employees were grandfathered in from the old plan. As these employees continue to retire, they are faced with extremely delicate financial decisions regarding pension plan distributions.

There are various pension payout options one can choose from in a traditional scenario (note that every situation is not identical). For this scenario we will assume this is a one-time decision with no pop-up provisions and only one beneficiary can be selected.

Howie and Mike were faced with the following options:

	Pension (per month)	Survivor Benefit (per month)
Option 1	full: $3,000	$0
Option 2	reduced: $2,700	$1,350
Option 3	reduced: $2,400	$2,400

Based on my experience, roughly 75% of those married and faced with these choices select Option 3, regardless of any other factors. Let's break down what these options mean for either Mike or Howie:

- If he chooses Option 1, he maximizes his benefit while he is alive, but upon his death his wife gets *nada*.

- If he chooses Option 2, he receives $300 less per month (that adds up to a forfeiture of more than $100,000 over the course of a 30-year retirement, without factoring in investment growth) and provides a benefit for his wife upon his death.

- If he chooses Option 3, he receives $600 less per month (forfeiting more than $200,000 over a 30-year retirement, without investment growth), and he leaves behind a healthy pension for his wife.

Howie realizes that he can't leave Sally without retirement income should he pass away prematurely (bad choice of words—*premature* implies that we had a specific date of death planned and our demise came early). Mike, on the other hand, sees nothing wrong with taking care of himself and not worrying about his wife. (It is now required that a spouse sign off if you choose a full pension without a survivor benefit.)

After carefully reviewing his expected cost of living in retirement, Howie chooses Option 3 and is willing to scale back his retirement plans to make it work.

What we haven't yet considered is the potential demise of Sally prior to Howie. In this case, $600 per month has been forfeited to protect Sally, but now there is no Sally. Howie is stuck with a greatly reduced pension, which dies with him. (Remember, we only get to name one beneficiary at the time of the decision-making). In this case, for all its noble intentions, Option 3 proves to be the wrong choice (another example of emotional vs. intellectual decision-making).

The most economical way to approach this is to replicate the survivor benefit option privately. What I mean is this: choose Option 1 and look for a life insurance policy that provides the survivor a benefit of $2,400 per month for life. The costs of Term life insurance have declined over the years. It is unlikely that the costs of paying the policy premium would exceed the monthly reduction in pension. This means that upon your death, the survivor gets no pension. But the lump sum death benefit can provide that.

In addition to a less expensive way of funding the survivor benefit, you now have control. Should your spouse pass away first, you can either cancel the policy, thereby saving over $600 per month, or name a new beneficiary (your pension lives on).

Please consider all factors when making this very important decision. If you are not in the best of health and don't expect to qualify for inexpensive life insurance, you may be forced to choose Option 2 or 3. Also, in this case, if you choose Option 3 and then pass away a few years into retirement, the cost of providing the survivor benefit was small.

As always, see a qualified financial consultant to help you in this critical decision-making process. Also, don't wait until the last minute. It may be prudent to consider your options several years prior to retirement, when you are younger, healthier, and less likely to be paralyzed in making your decision by your looming retirement.

Give Me Income or Give Me Death

"If you're given a choice between money and sex appeal,
take the money. As you get older, the money will become
your sex appeal."

-Katherine Hepburn-

Sam and Dolores grew up during the Depression. They met at age fifteen and were married at nineteen. They were dedicated parents who raised two children, Elizabeth and Aaron.

Their loving daughter Elizabeth was married with three kids of her own and lived in Texas. They spoke with her about once a week and saw the grandkids on holidays when Elizabeth flew home. Their son Aaron lived with his significant other in California. They hadn't seen him in two years but still sent him care packages every so often.

Over the years, Sam and Dolores had saved and scrounged their dollars, generously spoiling the children but settling for a less luxurious lifestyle themselves. Living solely off their income from CDs and bonds, they were regulars at all the local banks. They enjoyed chasing the highest paying interest rates, opening new accounts, and receiving free toasters and coffee makers. They didn't consider themselves much in the way of investors. However, they *did* go to all the free seminars with financial advisors that included a lunch or dinner. (And they say that there's no such thing as a free lunch!)

The few pleasures they afforded themselves were small. Sam loved to indulge in ice cream and cold beer while Dolores splurged to have her remaining hair curled every other week.

Their daughter Elizabeth tried many times to convince them that their stubborn financial habits were silly and outdated. However, they weren't the type of parents to take advice from their own children.

The couple's quality time together consisted of coupon clipping and harassing the grocery store cashier when the items rang up at the wrong price. It was this favorite pastime that surprisingly led them to change their ways.

It was a humid Sunday afternoon in June when Sam and Dolores stopped at the Winn-Dixie supermarket. They came prepared with their budget, shopping list, and double coupons in tow. After twenty-five minutes of scouring the aisles for bargains, they approached the checkout line.

As the checker scanned the items, Sam's face suddenly turned bright red. It was his ice cream! Ringing in at $3.50 a gallon instead of two gallons for five dollars, the ice cream had pushed Sam and Dolores over budget. Humiliated that their coupon had expired and their budget was so tight, they asked the checker to void the purchase. They quietly packed up the rest of their groceries and retreated home.

This embarrassing scene ignited a conversation that led the couple to evaluate their options. That day marked the beginning of a much less stressful financial outlook for Sam and Dolores.

Professional Perspective

Most of us know a Sam and Dolores. Show them sympathy because they can't help themselves. They grew up in a difficult era and have never opened themselves to new ideas or discussions. They may be willing to undergo great inconveniences to save or earn a dollar—by chasing an extra quarter-of-a-percent interest or eating an "early bird" special on the other side of town—but they aren't willing to entertain other ways of investing money that would make a far greater difference in their lives.

When it comes to money, look out! They have accounts at ten different banks, CDs galore, and a few stocks that they have held for the past 25 years. Ask them to talk about their stocks and you'll hear similar stories. "I bought that at $30 and it's quadrupled since." Now, ladies and gentlemen, quadrupling your money over the past 25 years equates to an average annual return of about 6% (that's five percentage points per year below the S&P 500). "Quadruple" has a wonderful ring to it, but we are not talking about a wonderful investment.

Over the years, my partner and I have faced this situation time and time again. Persuading the Sams and Doloreses of the world to change their ways often felt like a hopeless uphill battle—that is, until we designed TEDI™.

TEDI™—"Tax Efficient Distributions of Income"—is our patent-pending model that illustrates an effective, modern way of investing money in retirement with the aim of distributing income on a periodic basis while minimizing income tax implications. I know that's a mouthful, but the theory is relatively simple. It rests on the basic assumption that the longer you can stay invested, the more you can earn on a risk-adjusted basis. The key, as detailed in the illustration below, is in creating several different pools of money. Each pool represents a specific time frame for when the money will be needed.

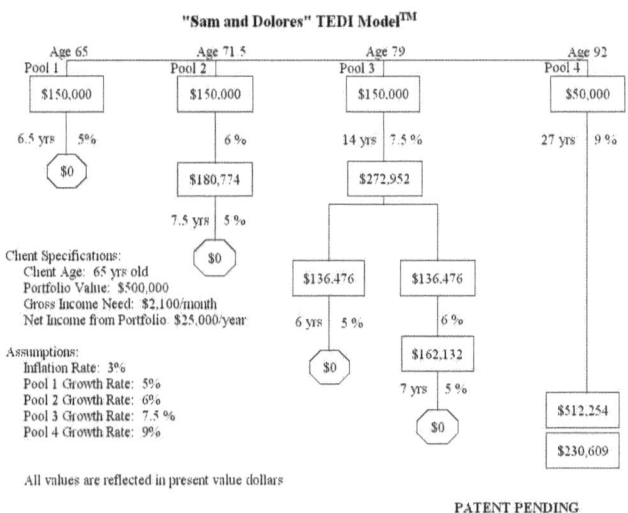

Pool #1 represents the money we need today. These are very stable investments that work to supply a steady stream of income for a number of years. When this pool of money becomes exhausted (including all income and principle), pool #2 takes its place. Meanwhile, pool #2 had been earning at a higher rate of return because we've been able to tie up this money for a longer pre-determined time period. (Generally, the longer you're willing to relinquish access to your money, the higher interest rates you can get.) For pool #2, we can assume higher growth rates, reinvestment of dividends, and best of all, the power of compounding—sometimes referred to as the Eighth Wonder of the World (at least by financial advisors—maybe we should get out more). Market volatility for the next four years is replaced with predictability (because income is made up of principle being paid out along with the fixed rate of return it is generating). The volatility is shifted to pools 3 and 4, which we won't need for a while. The goal is that we never have to pull money out when the market is down.

By using the principle in the designated early pools while reinvesting all income or growth in the later pools, we work to achieve a higher overall rate of return on our portfolios.

TEDI™ takes into account the impact of inflation, the Required Minimum Distribution of IRAs, and all other qualified (retirement) accounts. It also helps to fulfill the desire of most retirees to leave behind a legacy.

While TEDI™ is our approach to this scenario, it is not the only approach. Regardless of the direction you take, you need to take into account the following basic considerations:

- A diversified portfolio
- The impact of inflation on income
- Life expectancy
- Desire to create a legacy
- Taxes

For people like Sam and Dolores, retiring on the interest from CDs and bonds may not cut it anymore. TEDI™ isn't an investment or a product—it's a strategy for predictability and risk minimization. Sam and Dolores were able to find some peace of mind after meeting with us, and buy ice cream whether or not it was on sale.

I'm Confident I Have No Idea If I Can Ever Retire

"Anyone who lives within their means suffers from a lack of imagination."

-Oscar Wilde-

Boy, the headlines in the newspaper really made Jeremy feel great about his family's financial prospects. If the papers weren't talking about Social Security running out of money they were predicting the housing market was going to fall apart. He felt like he was born in the wrong generation—there was no way he was going to be able to plan a sound financial future for himself and his wife and children.

His parents and grandparents had the safety nets of corporate pensions, retiree health benefits, and Social Security. Added to that, they had the housing boom and saw the value of their homes go up by a zillion percent. He, on the other hand, had a 401(k) to manage while the headlines blared endlessly about a bankrupt Social Security trust fund. He bought his first home at the height of the housing bubble.

Jeremy wondered if any of his peers were able to save much. When he was a kid, he came home from school and played in the neighborhood. That was free. His kids had planned activities every afternoon from dance lessons to soccer practice to private tennis lessons. All of that cost money. He learned to play tennis with his friends on the courts at the local school. He had to belong to a private club to play now.

While he and his friends were playing in the neighborhood, someone's mother was always around paying attention and offering snacks. Everyone today had nannies or scheduled babysitters. If he and his wife wanted to go out on Saturday night, the cost of the babysitter was more expensive than the entertainment. How was he supposed to save for the kids' college educations (which were projected to be some astronomical figure by the time his kids were ready) and save for retirement as well?

He found himself eyeing sports cars the way he used to look at them in magazines as a kid. What was the point of being "responsible" and putting as much money as possible into his 401(k)? Maybe he'd buy himself a Porsche. And why work 80 hours a week, fishing for pay raises and benefits, when he could leave early on Fridays and spend more time fishing for catfish. With the way things were going, he'd never be able to retire and do these things so he may as well enjoy himself now.

Professional Perspective

Younger people starting their careers and families face many uncertainties. They feel they will never be able to make headway in planning for their family's security and a comfortable retirement. Many of the concerns they face are valid, but let's not forget that each era has presented a new set of hurdles.

The generation now in their eighties lived through the Depression and World War II. The generation now in its fifties faced home mortgage interest rates upwards of 15% as well as double-digit inflation. People of this generation never felt they would be able to afford home ownership. The Baby Boomers now in their mid-forties, fifties, and sixties faced intense competition for everything since there were so many of them vying for college entrance, jobs, and houses. At one point teachers couldn't find a job. Now there is tremendous demand for them. Everything changes.

Planning and making some intelligent assumptions about the future without predicting that the sky is falling is probably better than giving up and buying a Porsche (although not nearly as much fun).

I couldn't begin to theorize where Social Security is headed. On the one hand, I can't imagine a politician allowing it to fall apart. On the other hand, with all the Baby Boomers retiring and a shrinking workforce able to contribute, it is hard to figure out where the money is going to come from. Certain industries, such as the airline industry, are giving up their traditional defined pension plans to government bailout programs. From a personal planning point of view, conservative people may want not to include Social Security income in their retirement planning. In that way, anything that they *do* get will be a bonus.

Making retirement projections requires other assumptions, too—inflation rates, investment growth rates, and tax rates. The picture of your future may look rosy or bleak depending on the numbers used for these variables. For example, if you assume that inflation will be 2% and your investments will grow at 15%, your projected retirement will include second homes and world travel. If, on the other hand, you assume that inflation will be 5% and your investments will grow at 8%, you may feel moved to dust off your burger-flipping skills.

Neither extreme scenario will give you an accurate picture of what may happen. There are types of analyses that an advisor can do for you, which will build in various assumptions and project income levels. These statistical computer programs should give you a greater level of confidence about where your retirement is headed. By starting this type of planning at a young age the chances of a comfortable retirement are far greater.

Generations X and Y may commonly live to 90, 100, or 110. If that's the case, retiring in the traditional 55 – 65 age bracket will not be reasonable. Imagine trying to support a fifty-year retirement. More likely, the average retirement age will be 75. Social Security benefits may be similarly delayed.

Retirement Planning—Quick Recap

Social Security

- When deciding at what age to start drawing Social Security, take into account life expectancy, income need, and projected return on your investments. Working part-time and investing your Social Security benefits may prove to be a better move than waiting for higher benefits at a more advanced age.

- You need to assess honestly how much money you require to support your lifestyle before you can make a realistic retirement plan. Take the time to track your spending over several months. Often our spending habits are quite different from what we assume.

- Then take a stab at budgeting, adjusting after a few months for actual vs. budget discrepancies.

- The harsh reality is that younger members of the work force may be paying into a Social Security system that will be of little use to them in retirement (will the system even be there?). Take this into account when making your retirement savings plan.

Home

- For those nearing retirement who are asset rich but cash poor, the time may come to sell your home, downsize, and invest the difference to produce additional income. However, a reverse home mortgage is one option worth considering.

Pension

- You may be better off opting to receive full pension benefits, foregoing a survivor benefit for you spouse, and finding a life insurance policy on your own.

Smart Investing

- One way to help make sure your money lasts you through retirement is to divide it into separate pools. One pool can be put into short-term, stable investments to help provide a steady stream of income for a number of years. The other pools, meanwhile, can be earning on average a higher rate of return due to the longer-term nature of the investments. When the first pool dries up, switch to the second, and so on. Let compounding be your best friend and keep you sleeping soundly at night.

ESTATE PLANNING

Investments
and Financial Planning

GLASBERGEN

"I retire on Friday and I haven't saved a dime.
Here's your chance to become a legend!"

"Will" You "Trust" Me?

"There are people who have money,
and people who are rich."

-Coco Chanel-

Elaine and four of her friends had been playing canasta on Wednesdays for nearly twenty-five years. Over the years, they talked about, planned for, cried over, and analyzed every life event. No subject was left untouched—the five women were a tried and true support system for each other. They also were each other's primary source of information on all subjects, from the name of a skilled housepainter to where to go for good Chinese food to how to handle money and marriage issues. The five of them sat in the waiting room together when Phyllis's husband, Bob, had his bypass surgery. They agonized over how serious Anita was about the married dance instructor she'd been seeing. Once one of them found a good plumber or electrician, the other four became loyal customers. Some Wednesdays, life was fairly routine, in which case the friends played canasta seriously. Other weeks there was a serious issue to be dealt with, and not much card playing happened. On those occasions, the women usually settled on a plan of action before the afternoon was out.

Elaine always felt that she and her friends led very similar lives and had similar incomes and investments. They all had bought similar types of condominiums in similar types of developments. Over the years they had even done some traveling together. But when she left Shirley's that day, she was confused. The topic of conversation all through lunch had been the "living trusts" that both Shirley and her husband Sid, and Phyllis and her husband Bob, had just finished setting up.

To Elaine's way of thinking, trusts were for the *Lifestyles of the Rich and Famous* type of people. She and Irving had worked hard and lived modestly so they could enjoy a comfortable retirement. She didn't think they had the kind of money to have to be thinking about estate taxes, probate, or attorney's fees. But then again, she knew that Shirley and Phyllis didn't have vast amounts of money either, and two of the people she trusted most in the world had just set up revocable living trusts. All she and Irving had was a will that basically divided everything equally among their three children.

Not terribly sophisticated, Elaine tried to follow the conversation as much as she could so that she could explain it all to Irving when she got home. She didn't want to admit to her friends that she didn't understand much of what they were talking about or why they had done what they had done. Her head was spinning when she left Shirley's and she rushed right home so she could share all of this before it became even more muddled in her mind.

Professional Perspective

There's nothing funny about death. But you almost have to laugh at the decisions some of the most intelligent people make when preparing their estate for eventual transfer.

Figuring out an estate plan is confusing for most of us. There are two main schools of thought: draw up a simple will or create a revocable living trust.

The **simple will** serves as a mouthpiece for the deceased individual, expressing his or her wishes for disposing of the estate and its assets. It is inexpensive (relative to revocable living trusts) but it all too often leads to a probate situation at death, which can be costly and time consuming for the executor. The probate process in Florida, for example, could cost the estate between 3% and 7% on average, and take up to 18 months to finally settle. (Costs for probate differ dramatically by state—a professional should be consulted to advise you on your specific case.)

Revocable living trusts are initially more costly. However, they help avoid the likelihood that the heirs will have to undergo a probate process. Revocable trusts have many other benefits, as well. They can be set up to disburse assets to beneficiaries in various time frames, and they contain features that minimize estate taxes. Sometimes the choice is as simple as this: for an estate of $1 million, you could create a simple will for only $250, and potentially face probate costs of $30,000, or you could create a revocable living trust for $1,500 and avoid probate (and that $30,000 expense). Pay a little more now or a lot later.

There are some other differences besides cost between a will and a trust. The probate process is a court process and therefore everything that is filed becomes public record. Someone with less than scrupulous intentions can research the value of the estate and what each beneficiary receives. Also, while a will is being probated, an income tax return must be filed. Even if the process drags on for several years, the estate is still responsible for the yearly income tax until the estate is completely distributed.

Another thing to consider in estate planning is what would happen if you became incapacitated. A will does not spring to life until after death, while a revocable trust becomes effective upon signing and notarizing the document. If you have a will and someone needs to step in and manage your money for you, they will need to go to court and have the court appoint a conservator. If your assets are in trust, you and/or your co-trustee can immediately manage your money, pay your bills, etc.

Every situation is different, and of course this example is oversimplified, but the point is that trusts may be appropriate for anyone, however much or little money they have. A financial advisor and an estate attorney will analyze your circumstances and explain your options to you.

What's My Title?

"The difference between divorce and legal separation is that a legal separation gives a husband time to hide his money."

-Johnny Carson-

Valerie and Ken met through mutual friends and got involved fairly quickly. They were both in their fifties and divorced, with grown children from prior marriages. When you met them you could see how much they were enjoying each other's company. All their friends were happy for them. But after suffering through bad marriages and even worse divorces, neither was interested in planning a wedding anytime soon.

Valerie worked in an administrative position for a non-profit organization and Ken was a salesman for a construction materials company. Neither had an excessive income, and neither had much money accumulated, so it wasn't surprising that they began talking about moving in together. Soon they found a townhouse condominium that they both loved and—by pooling their money—they could afford.

Not having much money, Valerie and Ken didn't consider themselves the type of people to consult a financial advisor. (It's a misconception shared by many people.) Each time they had to make any type of financial decision, they did the best they could with the limited knowledge they had.

After they'd bought the condo, moved in, and set up their new home, Ken's son Nicholas came for a visit one weekend. He loved the new place and what they'd done with it, but he was surprised to find out that the townhouse was being held jointly as 'tenants-in-common.' Valerie and Ken had no idea what the implications of that were.

Nicholas liked Valerie, but couldn't help thinking of what might happen if (or rather when) she or his father passed away. Might Dad have to share the place with Valerie's kids, whom he'd never met? What if they couldn't afford the payments, or didn't want to pay them? Would they force his father to sell his share—basically evict him? And what would Nicholas do if he ended up owning the property with Valerie and she couldn't afford her share? What if Valerie wanted another man to move in with her?

The uncomfortable scenarios were endless....

Professional Perspective

How you title your assets will have an effect on your will, on your living trust, on whether or not your heirs owe estate taxes, as well as on some very practical living issues. The details of the different ways of titling assets vary depending upon your state of residence. I'll give you some general information here, but before you proceed with implementing any titling changes, you really should consult a financial advisor and/or an attorney in your state of residence.

In our example, Valerie and Ken held their townhouse as tenants-in-common. When property is held this way, each party owns a divided interest in the property. When one owner passes away, their proportionate share goes to whomever they have designated as beneficiaries in their will or trust. Valerie's children are her beneficiaries; Ken's children are his beneficiaries. Think about the implications of this. If Ken passes away first, Valerie owns one half of the townhouse, Ken's children own the other half. Valerie can't afford the mortgage by herself. Suppose she wants to continue to live there. How will Ken's children feel about continuing to pay his half of the mortgage, taxes, and other expenses? What if she doesn't get along with his children? Will they all be forced into being property holders together? It is recommended that language be included in your legal documents to address this issue if it pertains to your situation. This wasn't the ideal way to title this property.

The most common way to title jointly held property is "joint tenants with right of survivorship." When one person dies, his or her property will automatically transfer to the surviving party. Property held this way does not have to go through probate until the survivor passes away. The property owners do not have to be husband and wife and there can be more than two owners. One of the not-so-obvious uses of this type of titling is for a widowed parent with one child to hold an asset this way. When the widowed parent passes away, the asset will then automatically transfer to the child.

Some states are community property states—California, Arizona, and Texas, for example. In very general terms, property acquired during marriage is owned 50% by each spouse and therefore, upon the death of one spouse, 50% of the property passes to the deceased's estate.

If you set up a trust, the title on your assets should be changed to the trust's name. However, anything that is forgotten and left in an individual's or couple's name will then be subject to probate, and one of the benefits of having set up the trust will be negated. In one of the prior chapters we gave an example of a couple that had bank accounts and CDs all over town. In that chapter, chasing after one-quarter-of-a-percent interest was the issue. For the focus of this chapter, the downside of having accounts all over the place is the likelihood of forgetting to re-title all of your accounts if you decide that setting up a trust is the right way to go.

It's critically important that you get professional advice when determining the appropriate way to title any property. The implications of incorrectly titling an asset can be huge. It is also important to review how your assets are titled if you have a life-changing event or you move to another state where the laws may be different.

Which of My Kids Do I Like Best

"One of the reasons the rich get richer, the poor get
poorer, and the middle class struggles in debt is because
the subject of money is taught at home, not at school."

-Robert Kiyosaki-

Trudy and her husband, Saul, had been married for 30 years when her doctor told her that she had breast cancer. She was sixty years young. She and Saul had raised five children—two boys and three girls—and now that the kids were all grown, the two of them lived alone in the house they had lived in their entire married life. It was the house they raised their children in; they always thought of it as the house they would die in.

One night, as Trudy and Saul were eating and talking at the dinner table, they began to discuss updating their wills. They hadn't revised their wills at all since their oldest son was in high school and their youngest son was in elementary school. While they weren't wealthy by any means, they owned their house outright and Trudy did have some valuable jewelry that she wanted to be passed down to her children. Their financial situation had changed since the last will update. They agreed to go to their attorney on the following day.

Trudy's illness progressed rapidly over the next six months. The cancer eventually spread throughout her body. For those six months, Trudy was in and out of the hospital enduring chemotherapy treatments, and then, finally, she switched to hospice care. Trudy passed away one morning after she had spent time alone with each of her children and her husband. Her family was, of course, devastated by the loss, but they began to make funeral arrangements to finally lay Trudy to rest.

One year after his wife's death, Saul passed away in his sleep. While the doctor said he died of natural causes, his children believed that he died of a broken heart. Two funerals in such a short span had brought the five siblings together, but it didn't take them long to get past this sentiment and move on to arguing over the fact that the oldest of them, Keith, had been appointed as executor of their father's estate. The battle raged on between the children for more than two years. Screaming matches, court appearances, hurtful words, and silences were the only things the children shared with each other these days.

After the dust settled, no one in this once close family was actually speaking to each other. All of this chaos was due to the fact that one of the children had been named executor of the estate over the other four.

Professional Perspective

The job of the executor of an estate is to carry out the terms of the will. When the will is very explicit, as when the will defines specifically which piece of property goes to which heir, this may be a simple thing to do. When the will is broader and says, for example, that the property be divided equally among three children, the job of the executor can get complicated. Typically the various pieces of property must first be sold and then the proceeds are equally divided.

The process may be difficult and painful, but before choosing one child as executor, you need to examine the reality of the dynamics in your family. How well do the siblings get along? Do they trust each other? Who is most knowledgeable about legal matters? Who may have adequate time to put into managing the process? Who is careful with details? Who has the temperament to work with all the parties involved?

Let's say that there is a house that needs to be sold. Logic suggests that the sibling living in the same geographic area be chosen as executor. But what if he doesn't know anything about real estate and has never bought or sold property? It may not be very efficient for him to have to get up to speed on the process when his sister is more experienced. But what if she is really risk-averse and her brothers are sure that she'll sell to the first buyer and not get the best price? Before you know it, she's highly insulted that her family doesn't think she's a savvy businesswoman and her brother is hurt that he's been deemed incapable of doing the job. You can see that when money is involved, our best personality traits tend to go into hibernation.

To preserve family harmony, if for no other reason, it may be best to name an independent third party as executor (a common enemy to bind the siblings). Even if family harmony isn't at issue, if the executor of the estate is also a beneficiary, something in the terms of the will may result in a conflict of interest. The executor may be put in a position of having to decide between his or her own interests and the interests of the other beneficiaries. A large, complex estate should have an experienced, independent person handling the task. An attorney is the obvious first person to consider. This executor may have to be paid a fee, which is usually based upon the size of the estate.

Let Me Be

"Money is like an arm or leg—use it or lose it."

-Henry Ford-

Mary Jane was sweating as she sat in the conference room of my office. It wasn't the heat or the heavy sweatpants and sweatshirt she was wearing that made her perspire. It was, I learned, the fact that she'd been carrying a check for $250,000 in her pocketbook for the past week. She was beside herself with indecision, grief, anxiety, and guilt.

It had been almost a month since the accident. Roscoe had done the stunt more than a thousand times in front of live audiences. He was brilliant on the trapeze, sometimes even referred to as a master of his craft.

They had met nine years earlier in Oklahoma City. Roscoe had been touring with the circus for five years when Mary Jane walked into the tent where the team was running through its performance for that night's main event. Friends of the couple would later say it was love at first flight.

The trapeze had always fascinated Mary Jane. Men, on the other hand, had always frightened her. At 275 pounds, she had rarely drawn affectionate looks from strangers. So when Roscoe began walking in her direction, she considered escaping the tent and running all the way home. But when he motioned for her to follow him, she uncharacteristically followed. Mary Jane felt drawn to him—a sense of excitement and panic welled up inside of her.

Roscoe had an innate ability to reach out to people and connect with them. Back in high school, he would walk past the cheerleaders as if they weren't even there. He was always attracted to the girls with personality, regardless of their looks.

Roscoe sensed that there was something pure about Mary Jane. He was captured by her innocence and the look of awe on her face. Mary Jane recognized the skill and passion that he and his team brought to their work. He offered her front row tickets for that night's show.

That chance meeting changed both of their lives forever. After falling deeply in love and spending every spare minute they had together, and then some, they married two months later. That first night and for the next twelve years, Mary Jane was in the front row for every one of Roscoe's performances.

The accident occurred six weeks prior to their thirteenth wedding anniversary. When Roscoe's partner was swinging to reach for Roscoe's hand, he did the unthinkable: he missed. By the time Roscoe realized, he had already released himself from the trapeze he was swinging from. Roscoe crashed to the ground 100 feet below. His crushed and rumpled body was rushed to the hospital, but the damage was too severe. He was placed on life support. After performing all the relevant tests, the doctors declared him brain dead.

Mary Jane was devastated. The doctors explained the situation to her and left the fate of Roscoe in her hands. What was she to do? Roscoe had always made all the decisions for them. She knew Roscoe would not want to be kept alive by machines. She knew in her heart that his passion was performing on the trapeze. If he couldn't perform then he wasn't really living at all. After an agonizing week passed without any signs of improvement, she conceded it was over.

She was emotionally paralyzed when she received the $250,000 check from the insurance company. She had been advised by friends and family not to cash it because of the taxes she would pay. Three weeks and some bad advice later, with a check in her bag from the proceeds of Roscoe's life insurance policy, she paid me a visit.

Professional Perspective

Mary Jane was put in an unenviable position, one that I wouldn't wish on my worst enemy. Under pressing conditions, she was required to determine the fate of her beloved husband. A rational person may be able to weigh all the factors and come to a conclusion. But who on earth is rational at a time like that?

A **living will** should be a staple in everyone's estate plan. Often referred to as a "Dying with Dignity" document, it keeps the onus of decision-making with the patient, even when he or she is incapable of communication. This document should clearly express the patient's wishes should he or she ever be in Roscoe's position. This document can specify whether or not you want to remain on a respirator, and for how long; whether or not you want to receive food and water; whether or not you wish to be revived if your heart stops; and what to do in a number of other scenarios (including organ donation).

Mary Jane should never have had to make that decision. If Roscoe had a living will, his wishes would have been known to all—and granted. This would have relieved poor Mary Jane of the guilt she continued to feel after deciding to terminate Roscoe's life support.

In addition to a living will, some other key documents that you may want to consider as part of your estate plan are:

Simple Will—This document will serve as your mouthpiece upon your death. It explains to all parties involved exactly what you want done with all of your possessions.

Revocable Living Trust—This document serves as a will but with greater flexibility. It helps to avoid the probate process as well as potential estate taxes.

Pour Over Will—This document captures all the assets that are not part of the trust and essentially pours them into the Revocable Trust.

Durable Power of Attorney—This document names someone to step into your shoes to make financial decisions for you should you be unable to make them for yourself.

Health Care Surrogate—This document names someone to step into your shoes to make health care decisions for you should you not be able to make them for yourself.

The second unnecessary crisis that Mary Jane faced was that check for the startling amount of $250,000. Please recognize the difference between income tax and estate tax. If you are the owner of a life insurance policy, the policy is considered part of your estate for estate tax purposes. Roscoe was the owner and the insured party, so the proceeds from his insurance policies would not be considered taxable income to the beneficiary—they were part of his estate and figured into estate tax calculations. Mary Jane could have deposited the check the day she received it and avoided undue emotional hardship.

If Roscoe and Mary Jane's total estate value exceeded the maximum credit shelter, there may have been an estate tax due when filing the estate tax return. The full details of estate and estate tax planning are far too complex for the scope of this book. Without advice from a professional, it's quite possible that heirs may end up forfeiting exclusions and paying too much in taxes.

These are just some of the reasons to meet with a qualified financial consultant. Don't wait to address these issues. Fortunately or unfortunately, we do not have a crystal ball telling us when our time is up. It's important to have a solid estate plan in place to avoid putting your loved ones through stressful circumstances like Mary Jane's. The monetary expense is worth the comfort you will feel knowing that you have addressed some major difficulties on your own terms.

A Parent's Understudy

"There is always one moment in childhood when the door
opens and lets the future in."

-Graham Greene-

When it came to raising their children and managing their finances, they did everything by the book. They read to their children every day. They limited the junk food in the house and sat down as a family to eat dinner together every night. Jack helped coach the T-ball team and Sarah volunteered at the pre-school one day a week. They kept three months of living expenses in an emergency fund. Jack contributed the maximum to his 401(k). They paid off their credit card balance each month. They agreed on all of these things and their marriage was a smooth one with the exception of one issue.

Who would be the guardians of their children in the event that something happened to them?

Sarah wanted to name her sister and brother-in-law, Linda and Bob, as the children's guardians. Jack's response was, "Your sister is a flake. She'd never get a balanced meal on the table because she'd be too busy painting their faces or digging in the dirt. And Bob wouldn't know how to handle our money if his life depended on it. He'd buy them all the latest gadgets and they'd have no money for college."

Jack felt that his brother Sam would be perfect. Not only was Sam smart and responsible, but his girlfriend, Lucy, was a pre-school teacher. Sarah said, "You've got to be kidding. Sam is the most emotionally uninvolved man I've ever met. Sure, he'd take care of their money but he wouldn't know how to take care of THEM!! As for Lucy, she's just one of many girlfriends he's had. It's like a revolving door with him—and that's not the kind of education I want for the kids."

Jack's parents were in their early sixties, so by the time the kids were teens, they'd be in their seventies—not a great age for staying on top of teenagers. Jack wouldn't even discuss Sarah's mom as a possibility. He thought she was barely capable of taking care of herself since Sarah's dad had died, never mind taking care of two children.

The conversation ended at an impasse every time. The kids were now two and four and no provisions for them had been made.

Professional Perspective

This must be one of the most emotionally charged decisions parents have to make. Not only do we have to deal with our own mortality, but we also have to figure out who will best ensure the well being of our children if we are unable to do so. For many of us, there is no clear-cut right choice of whom to name as guardians. We may not be perfect parents ourselves, but it's still difficult to decide who will raise our children the way we want.

Some parents try to minimize risks by never booking themselves on the same airplane flight. In reality, most couples and families are in the car together on a routine basis, where the chances of something happening are far greater than a plane crash. Heading down the FDR Drive in Manhattan, or even cruising the streets of Del Ray Beach in Florida behind drivers who can barely peer over the steering wheel, is far riskier than taking a flight from Florida to New York!

When you're deciding whom to appoint as guardian, there are many factors to consider. For example:

- Who lives in the same geographic area? The children's lives may not need to be further disrupted by a move to a new part of the country.
- Who also has children? Someone who's already a parent will be accustomed to a parent's lifestyle and responsibilities, as opposed to a single person's lifestyle.
- Who has the same types of values and priorities as you?
- Whom do you trust to follow through on your wishes and directives?
- How old is the person? Your parents—as opposed to a sibling—may be getting too old to chase preschoolers or cope with teenage histrionics.

Not making a decision in this case is probably worse than making a less than perfect choice. If you don't name a guardian for your children, and something happens to you, the court will do it. A judge has no way of knowing the personalities, the values, or the dynamics of your or your spouse's family.

As difficult a decision as this is, you need to do it. Sit down in a room with pad and pen and list your options, with pros and cons for each. Come up with a first choice and then go speak with them. Make sure they are willing to take on this responsibility. This should *not* be a decision they find out about after the fact. If they don't want to be named guardian, go to your second choice and so on. Also, take into account close friends—a guardian does not need to be related. Your friends may actually live a lifestyle more similar to yours than do your relatives. That's probably why they are your close friends.

It also may make sense to consider appointing one party as guardian or caretaker, and put another party in charge of "the money" or financial decisions. This may offer some balance and compromise.

Know When to Hold 'Em and Know When to Fold 'Em

"Money doesn't talk, it swears."

-Bob Dylan-

Bob and Brenda were "townies." They grew up in Springfield, U.S.A., went to the local public schools, and had part-time jobs around town growing up. Brenda went on to get her Associates Degree at Springfield Community College while Bob began working full-time at the grocery store he had been working at through high school. They both continued living at home during this time to save money for the down payment on a house. Once Brenda earned her degree and got a job as a teacher's assistant, they got married.

Their first home was a little two-bedroom cottage not more than a mile from where they had grown up. Bob worked hard at the grocery store and soon got promoted to one of the department managers. Brenda became pregnant with their first child. Before they knew it, they had two children and Bob was the Springfield store manager. Things were going just as they had always planned—which usually means life has a little surprise up its sleeve.

Bob had a quirky aunt who had never married. She lived in Springfield, too, but stayed pretty much to herself. Bob would visit periodically and always went over to shovel her walkway after a snowstorm or to fix a leaky pipe. He really didn't know much about her, nor did he think they had a very close relationship.

One day, the Chief of Police, with whom he had gone to high school, called to tell him that his aunt had passed away. It appeared that she had died peacefully in her sleep two nights before. After the funeral, Bob received a phone call from an attorney in town asking him to come in for a meeting. Bob soon found out that his quirky maiden aunt had quite a bit of money squirreled away—and had left it all to him.

Bob and Brenda felt like they'd hit the lottery. Never in a million years did they think they would ever have this kind of money. First they each bought a new luxury car, next they bought some jewelry, and then they took the honeymoon they never could afford. When they got back, they found that news had traveled fast around their small town. It seemed that everyone knew the details of their inheritance. Old friends and relatives alike started coming to their door to tell them about their money problems and to ask for "loans." Bob felt like the Godfather and began handing out money and advice.

Next, Bob and Brenda decided that their small home wasn't right for their newfound status. They bought a large piece of land at the edge of town and started to work with an architect to design a huge house. The plans called for everything from a swimming pool to an elevator to second floor balconies out-side each bedroom. Construction began and, as with all building projects, problems arose and costs went up. The money was flying out the door fast enough to make Bob and Brenda's heads spin. Bob had given up his job at the grocery store, and Brenda had stopped working when the kids were born, so while all the money was going out nothing was coming in.

Two years later the house *still* wasn't done. Bob and Brenda were quickly run-ning out of money and they were desperate to move in. Luckily for them, the town building inspector was an old friend and gave them a Certificate of Occupancy even though they should not have been able to move in yet. They were now living in their house but had no more money to do the landscaping, and the neighbors weren't happy.

One morning Brenda went out to get the mail. Bob saw her face as she came into the house and asked her what was wrong. She told him that their 2006 property tax bill had arrived, and showed him the number. He turned as pale as she was. Not being very sophisticated about money, they had never researched the costs associated with maintaining a lifestyle like this.

The next morning, Bob swallowed his pride and went to talk to the people he still knew at the grocery store to see about getting his job back.

Professional Perspective

We've all read the stories or watched the segments on the television news mag-azines that look up lottery winners five years later. It's amazing the number of recent millionaires that are now in bankruptcy. Getting a large, unexpected inheritance can be much the same as winning the lottery—wonderful if it is handled properly, a nightmare if it isn't.

Did Bob's quirky aunt hurt the family or help it by leaving him a pile of cash? Unfortunately, many people who come into large sums of money don't have the tools or experience to know how to make it last. Some, like Bob and Brenda, spend like crazy until they "suddenly" have nothing left. Others recognize that they don't know how to handle this kind of money and seek professional help.

If you are planning your estate and you're not sure how the recipient(s) of your money are going to handle it, the better idea may be to take this into account in your estate plan.

An **estate planning attorney** is the person to lead you through the complexities of wills, trusts, gifts, and estate taxes.

As discussed earlier, the advantage of setting up a trust is that its creator can have some control over the management of his or her assets even after death. The trust can be set up so that portions of the income and/or the assets are passed on to the beneficiary at predetermined points in time—usually when the beneficiary reaches certain ages, graduates from college, etc. This way, the creator of the trust can ensure that a beneficiary inexperienced in handling money doesn't have access to the inheritance all at once (and therefore can't lose it all at once).

A trust can also be set up with an attorney, bank, or trust department as trustee as opposed to a family member. This independent professional has the fiduciary responsibility to administer the trust appropriately. He or she will be less likely to let emotion get involved with decisions regarding the money.

If you can teach your beneficiaries (e.g. your children) how to handle money, that's probably the most prudent course of action. But sometimes it isn't enough. Whether you have a Bob-and-Brenda or a Jackpot Judy in your family, you can set up proper boundaries in your estate plan to protect your assets—and protect your beneficiaries from themselves.

Estate Planning—Quick Recap

Wills and Trusts

- A simple will is cheaper than a revocable living trust in the short run, but may prove more costly in probate court.

- Trusts may be appropriate for anyone, not just the extremely wealthy.

- Families can be torn apart by inheritance disputes, particularly when one sibling has been given the power of executing the will.

- If the executor of a will is also a beneficiary, the terms of the will may lead to a conflict of interest, or at least the appearance of one.

- Sometimes the best strategy is to appoint a neutral third party as executor.

- Creating a living will, a durable power of attorney, and a health care surrogate allows you to face difficult decisions about your healthcare and your finances now so that your wishes will be known and carried out should you become incapacitated.

- Trusts can help ensure that a beneficiary inexperienced in handling money gets access to an inheritance in stages (or any other method you choose).

Titles

- How you title your assets can have major unintended consequences.

- There are different ways to title jointly held property—make sure you understand the implications of each.

- After a life-changing event or a move to a different state, you should review the titles of your assets to see if you need to make changes.

- Before re-titling, consult a financial advisor or an attorney. Property and inheritance laws vary from state to state.

Naming a Guardian

- Not choosing a guardian for your children is worse than choosing a guardian whom you consider less than perfect.

- Remember to consider close friends—guardians need not be relatives.

TAX PLANNING

"After federal, state, and local taxes, you get one-third of a wish."

Bring Home the Bacon

"You don't pay taxes—they take taxes."

-Chris Rock-

Ken is a 42-year-old construction worker. He spends long and dusty days in the hot Florida sun building and rebuilding roads, highways, and overpasses. He started in construction when he was about 18 in order to support his young wife and the child they were expecting at the time. Since then, Ken has moved around to a couple of different positions and is currently a jackhammer operator. Moving from position to position usually involved some kind of a pay increase.

Ken remembers when he received his first paycheck. He recalls the broad smile that spread across his face when he looked at the pay stub and saw his gross salary. He also remembers that smile fading as his gaze shifted to the lines of deductions and to the final, much-reduced number. He remembers thinking, who is this FICA guy, anyway, and why does he get a big chunk of my hard-earned money?

Twenty-four years later, Ken is still working in construction, but he is making quite a bit more money now than when he first started. A combination of cost-of-living pay increases, bonuses, and raises has definitely elevated Ken's gross salary over the years. The part that Ken just can't get over is that the more he makes, the more of his salary he seems to lose to FICA and taxes. His frustration level over his tax situation is mounting. It almost seems to him that it doesn't even make sense to bust his butt every day working like a dog in the heat, because a great portion of his income just goes to the government anyway.

When he stopped into my office he was on the verge of quitting the field that had been his sole source of income for his entire working life. In Ken's head, he'd truly convinced himself that it would be cheaper for him just to give up working overtime all together than to continue working to pay more taxes to the government.

Professional Perspective

Unfortunately, Ken did not understand how he was being taxed on his income. He was under the false impression that for every additional dollar he made, the same percentage ended up in the hands of Uncle Sam. He's not alone—taxes are one of those subjects everyone knows they should better understand but can't really bring themselves to make the effort. Not only are they confusing but the rules are constantly changing, so it is impossible for the average person to feel comfortable that their knowledge is still accurate. Your tax advisor can educate you about FICA—made up of Social Security (which has a cap) and Medicare (which doesn't have a cap on the amount of tax you can pay).

One of the key tax concepts that Ken didn't grasp is the fact that all of our income is not taxed at the same rate. Tax advisors refer to the "effective tax rate," which is actual income tax paid divided by the net taxable income. The basic idea is that tax rates progressively increase as income increases, but the rate increases by brackets. *Within* a bracket, rates do not increase with an increase in income—only when our income jumps to the next bracket does the tax rate go up. The chart (from IRS tax tables) below illustrates this:

Married Filing Jointly or Qualifying Widow(er) Filing Status (as of 2006)

- 10% on the income between $0 and $15,100
- 15% on the income between $15,100 and $61,300; *plus* $1,510.00
- 25% on the income between $61,300 and $123,700; *plus* $8,440.00
- 28% on the income between $123,700 and $188,450; *plus* $24,040.00
- 33% on the income between $188,450 and $336,550; *plus* $42,170.00
- 35% on the income over $336,550; *plus* $91,043.00

To use Ken as an example, he is married and files a joint tax return. His current income is $70,000 per year. But that is not the figure that the tax rates refer to. The income levels in the chart above refer to "taxable income." This means that your tax rate is based on your income after you deduct non-taxable income, itemized deductions/standard deductions, personal exemptions, etc. Ken's taxable income is $60,000 per year. His tax rate is 10% on the first $15,100 of income and then 15% on the balance. By reducing his taxable income, he kept his marginal tax rate at 15% instead of 25%. He returned to his long hours of jackhammering with a lighter heart (and thick earplugs).

As you can see in the chart, managing your taxable income can really be to your benefit. Some people shift their investments into municipal bonds to try to lower their taxable income and keep from moving into the next marginal tax bracket. Using all the itemized deductions available to you is also critical. Other ways of reducing your taxable income include contributing to IRAs or 401(k)'s. Your tax advisor can also indicate potential AMT (alternative minimum tax) situations. This tax has had an increasing impact on the average payer.

Taxes are complicated. Even though your neighbor Sid tells you he can explain how to develop a tax smart strategy for you, it is probably in your best interest to consult with a tax advisor before proceeding. Everybody's specific situation is different and it is a professional's job to keep current with this ever-shifting subject.

Anything But Ordinary

"I have enough money to last me the rest of my life, unless
I buy something."

-Jackie Mason-

Diana was an impulse buyer. Her buying habits went far beyond purchasing a stick of gum, magazines, and batteries at the checkout counter; she'd buy the outfit in the storefront window, matching earrings, and maybe a purse or two for good measure. Diana's weekends were never complete without a visit to the mall. She was a two-bagger—one hand Nine West, the other Gap. While she and her girlfriends enjoyed the ride, they paid the monthly price.

When the mail came and VISA, MasterCard, or American Express marked the outside of an envelope, Diana felt physically ill. On several occasions, the feeling actually made her contemplate kicking her shopping addiction, but she never officially did so. Instead, she played the balance transfer game as well as anyone. She was constantly moving balances from one card to another to minimize the interest charges. The lowest interest rate charge Diana could receive was 7%.

Her total credit card debt toppled over the $4,000 mark. Yet she continually managed to rationalize her obsession. After all, she was a single woman with a decent paying job and a budding career in telecommunications. She felt she was entitled to a few perks. If not now, when would she be? Besides, she was 32, and two blind dates a month for a year and a half had not led to one solid candidate. The prospect of getting married in the near future was not looking good. She might as well treat herself.

Despite being an admitted shopaholic, Diana still managed to pay herself first and hold on to some of her financial dignity. She maintained $10,000 in her savings account. The initial $100 of every biweekly paycheck went into the company 401(k) retirement plan. The next $50 she had deposited in her Roth IRA that systematically bought into a tax-free municipal bond fund. In addition, she electronically transferred $200 per month from her checking account to her non-retirement brokerage account where she purchased her stocks.

She had grand plans for the latter account. She would need $1,200 for a quarter-share in a Jersey shore house next summer. But more importantly, within the next three years she hoped to move out of her Staten Island apartment and purchase a small two-bedroom townhouse in Brooklyn Heights with her friend Amy.

Of course, Diana purchased investments like footwear. She'd buy four at a time, take them home, wear them around the house for a while, and then return three. The stocks she kept sat in her account like shoes on a rack. Her research consisted of water-cooler talk, financial magazine recommendations, and her dad's boasting of "sure-fire" winners.

After meeting with her accountant each year, she was shocked at the amount of taxes she owed on April 15th. Her accountant advised her as to how much she needed to withhold from each paycheck to avoid owing money every year. Inevitably, Uncle Sam was knocking on the door for more.

For our first meeting, I asked her to bring copies of all her investment account statements for the past year. She could not be faulted for lack of organizational skills. Diana even maintained a clever financial fashion sense of sorts. She arrived with a blue binder for 401(k) statements, a red one for Roth IRA's, and a green binder for her non-retirement account statements. She kept each set of documents neatly hole-punched and tabbed, with dividers that were a reminder of the loose-leaf paper from school days.

It took only minutes to uncover the cause of her tax woes.

Professional Perspective

Does anyone like paying taxes? Deep down, we know that our tax money pays for our children's education, our hospitals, services for the poor, etc.... But we'd much rather someone else foot the bill. There's another way to look at it, of course: when you think about it, if you are paying a lot of tax, it usually means you are making a lot of money. As my father-in-law always says, no one is in the 100% tax bracket. Every dollar earned is still more than you had before, regardless of what percentage of it ends up in your pocket.

The government has put a taxing procedure in place and it is our job to manage the system as best as possible. If they are willing to give us a tax break, we need to take advantage of it. Diana was afforded the opportunity to participate in her company's 401(k) retirement plan. This plan allows her to shelter $15,000 of income (the limits for 2006) from taxation. This money can grow tax-deferred until she is 70 ½, at which point she would be required to start taking distributions according to life expectancy tables.

To put this in perspective, if Diana is in the 28% federal income tax bracket (we will ignore state and city taxes for this example), for every $100 she puts into her 401(k), she only gets taxed on $72 in her paycheck. This is quite an incentive to save. Over thirty years, that $100 per paycheck contribution (26 paychecks per year), compounded at 7% annually, will total over $260,000. If she still has a taste for shoes by then, she can give Imelda Marcos a run for her money.

Since the earnings within her 401(k) are not taxable until she withdraws them, Diana can buy and sell investments without any tax implications, as well as earn and reinvest dividend income without tax considerations.

She will be taxed at her ordinary income tax bracket when she does finally withdraw money from that account after age 59 ½. However, one would expect to be in a lower income tax bracket during retirement than while employed, thereby justifying delaying the tax consequence and enjoying the benefits of compounding.

The Roth IRA has some similarities to the 401(k). Both retirement vehicles allow for earnings without annual tax implications. However, the maximum Roth IRA contribution per year is $4,000 (in 2006) and it is not tax deductible, but the funds grow tax-free forever and can be withdrawn after 59 ½. There are many restrictions and eligibility factors regarding IRA contributions. It's best to consult with a tax advisor before making a contribution.

Diana's non-retirement account has the most flexibility since she can access the funds at her discretion. But it does not provide many tax benefits.

Diana handled most of her finances correctly. Saving money alone put her far ahead of most of her peers. She also realized that the best way to save money was systematically. This strategy is referred to as "dollar-cost-averaging".

Diana's tax problems were a result of her choice of investment within the various accounts. The following summarizes the source of these problems:

1.   She bought and sold regularly in her non-retirement account. This resulted in short term capital gains that were taxed at her ordinary income tax bracket (28%). Had she held these investments for more

than one year, she would have been taxed at the long-term capital gains rate of only 15% (as of 2006).

2.   She should have done her buying and selling within her Roth IRA. There would have been no tax consequence to her actions within this account.

3.   She bought tax-free municipal bonds in her Roth IRA. The Roth IRA already enjoys tax-free growth. Buying tax-free municipal bonds means she was sacrificing yield for tax freedom she was already receiving. She could have purchased high-grade corporate taxable bonds and realized higher annual returns.

Here is a little more advice for Diana (and others who share her impulses):

1.   She needs to eliminate her credit card debt. She was earning 3% in interest on the $10,000 in her savings account but was paying 7% interest on her $4,000 in credit card debt. She should use her savings account to pay off the credit cards. She would be saving a sizeable amount per year.

2.   She should consider purchasing less volatile investments within her non-retirement brokerage account. Diana was planning on buying the townhouse within three years. A downturn in the market could seriously impact her ability to do so. She does not want to take on too much risk with her money with such a short-term goal on the horizon. More aggressive saving and capital preservation are most appropriate here.

Defer or Not to Defer

"The IRS! They're like the Mafia, they can take anything they want!"

-Jerry Seinfeld-

Regina started working when the law said she could, at the age of 16. While she was completing her tax paperwork for the company to make deductions from her check, she became overwhelmed and confused. The Human Resources lady explained the different tax deductions she could choose from, basically letting her know that she could choose to have them take more taxes out of her check up front or take less taxes up front. To Regina, the logical choice was to have them take less in taxes up front, so that she would have more money to spend in the here and now.

It's been quite a few years since her first job. Now Regina is working full-time for a local caterer, making about three times the amount that she was making at her first job. She is in her late twenties, she's never been married, and doesn't have any children. She has as little as possible taken out of her paycheck, believing that this is the best strategy for paying taxes over the long haul. She still operates on the theory that it is better to have more money now, not later.

Lately, though, Regina is starting to question this strategy. It seems like every year when she prepares her tax returns she always has to write a fat check to the IRS. Why doesn't she ever get a refund check from the government like all of her co-workers? They are always using their refund checks to go on vacations or put down payments on new cars. For once, she would like to receive money from the IRS instead of having to pay.

Professional Perspective

Contrary to what you might think, your accountant is not doing you any great favors when you get a large tax refund. In fact, what's happening is that you've been giving Uncle Sam a yearlong interest-free loan out of your paycheck. On the other hand, planning on a refund can be a good approach if you don't have the discipline to save enough to pay Uncle Sam come April 15th.

The amount that is withheld from your paycheck is based upon what you've filled out on your W-4, a form we've all stared at blankly at some point. The scenario usually is this. It's our first day at a new job. We've been up since who knows when, terrified that we'd oversleep. As a matter of fact, we woke up a number of times during the night, sure that our alarm clock wasn't working. The first cup of coffee was at 6:30 AM and when the Human Resource lady asked if we'd like coffee, we wanted to be polite so we're drinking cup number three at 9:15 AM. Now she's sat us down in a cubby with a stack of forms to fill out. Our hands are a little sweaty from coffee and nerves and we start to plug away. We've finally made our way to the last document in the pile—the W-4. Our eyes start to glaze over as we read about exemptions, dependants, and allowances. At that point, unable to figure out if we're double-counting the kids, we stick something on the little lines and just hope for the best. We then start our new job and never think about withholding taxes again.

The more dependants claimed on the W-4, the less tax withheld from your paycheck. The assumption is that you will have more personal exemptions to reduce your taxable income. In a perfect world, you would be able to figure out the exact number to put in so that the perfect amount would be withheld. That's impossible to do. Many people love to get a refund when they file their income taxes. Their mind-set is that it's like a bonus or found money. In reality, it is your hard-earned money that the government has been using for free all year. You're not getting extra money; you're getting your own money back.

If you're disciplined enough to plan and save, the better scenario is to have less money withheld all year so you can use it and/or invest it. Then, come tax time, you can accurately calculate your taxes and pay the government what you owe. This way, you've had the use of your money all year long. There is a potential downside to this approach. If you owe money come April 15th, you have to have the cash available to pay what you owe. If you know yourself well enough to know you won't put the money aside on your own, this isn't the approach for you.

I don't know if anyone goes back to Human Resources and reviews their W-4's. It's a document that should be revised when there has been a change such as a new baby, or when a child is no longer a dependant. It also should be reviewed if you find you are either getting a large refund or that you owe a lot. A tax professional may be able to review your specific situation and assist you with making some logical adjustments—it may even be appropriate to schedule a mid-year evaluation with your accountant to see if adjustments are needed.

Tax Planning—Quick Recap

Bracketeering

- Tax rates progressively increase as income increases, but the rate increases by brackets. Accountants refer to your "effective tax rate"—the amount of income tax paid divided by your taxable income. An increase in income *within* a bracket will not increase the tax rate (see IRS tax tables at www.irs.gov).

- Managing your taxable income can be to your benefit. By using all available itemized deductions, and by contributing to IRA's and 401(k)'s, you may be able to keep yourself in a lower tax bracket.

The Right Account

- If you buy and sell stocks frequently within a retirement account, the transactions are not taxable events. But if you do this in a non-retirement account, you'll face potential short-term capital gains taxes (taxed at your income bracket). Instead, hold onto a stock for a year in this account and when you sell it you will owe the much lower long-term capital gains tax of 15%.

- To achieve a short-term earnings goal (for a major purchase, for example), choose less volatile investments in your non-retirement account and save aggressively. More aggressive positions in your portfolio may be more appropriate in tax-sheltered retirement accounts.

Withholding Praise

- Tax refunds aren't all they're cracked up to be. If you can trust yourself to put money aside to pay taxes each spring, why not have the use of your money all year round instead of loaning it to the government interest-free?

CHOOSING A FINANCIAL ADVISOR

"They chose those two animals to represent the stock market because your broker will feed you all the bull you can bear."

Credentials

"A fool and her money are soon courted."

-Helen Rowland-

Barbara and Mel had always taken care of their own finances. Now that they were in their late fifties, however, they weren't sure if they were knowledgeable enough to manage the amount of money they had accumulated. They also wanted to ensure that they were well positioned for retirement. It seemed that they had reached the point of turning to a professional.

They weren't the kind of people to open the yellow pages and pick the biggest ad or the first name they found—they wanted to know something about the financial advising profession before making their choice. They started their research by gathering names of advisors that their friends used, that they heard referenced in the media, or that seemed to be actively involved in the community.

Everyone seemed to have a different list of initials after their names! Articles they read detailed the differences between a stockbroker and an advisor. Some advisors had no initials after their name—what did that imply? Barbara and Mel were looking for someone to manage their investments, so did they care that someone was licensed to sell insurance? What was a Series 7 anyway?

After a long afternoon spent trying to understand fiduciary responsibility and what the "prudent investor concept" was, Barbara and Mel decided what they really needed was a drink.

Why was this so complicated? After all, when they needed medical attention the credential they cared about was that the doctor was Board Certified in his or her specialty. When they needed an electrician, they made sure he was licensed and insured. And when they needed the services of an attorney, they looked to see that the lawyer had passed the bar and was licensed in their state.

But what about CFP®, RIA, MBA, CLU, CLTC, CSA…what did all this mean?

Professional Perspective

The financial services profession is comprised of many different segments, which partly explains the proliferation of specialties and the (initially) confusing array of certifications.

First of all, let's look at what a few of the most common abbreviations mean (this list is not all-inclusive).

- A CFP® is a **Certified Financial Planner**™. This means that he or she has taken a series of courses in different segments of finance, such as investments, taxes, insurance, and estate planning. Certified Financial Planners™ have passed standardized exams in each of these sections as well as a comprehensive exam at the end of the coursework. The CFP® board also requires a certain amount of work experience. The planner must adhere to a Code of Ethics and there is an oversight/disciplinary board to deal with violations.

- RIA stands for **Registered Investment Advisor,** which means that this person is registered with the Securities and Exchange Commission (SEC). An IAR is an **Investment Advisor Representative** that works through an RIA. There is no educational requirement to become an IAR.

- MBA stands for **Masters in Business Administration**. This means this person has completed two years of graduate level work in business.

- RFC stands for **Registered Financial Consultant.** Several courses must be taken and passed before a person can sit for the comprehensive CFP® exam. RFCs have taken and passed those classes, regardless of whether or not they have passed the CFP® exam.

- A CLTC is a **Certified Long Term Care** specialist. This is a fairly new designation that requires detailed coursework in the field of long-term care insurance. Not a required certification, it will nonetheless let you know that the person you are dealing with is knowledgeable in this field.

- CSA is a **Certified Senior Advisor**. This is also a fairly new designation that requires coursework and testing. Financial advisors specializing in working with the elderly may have this designation. It indicates that they are knowledgeable in the areas of Medicare, Medicaid, geriatric care management, elder law, etc.

Everyone's specific requirements from an advisor are different. There are lots of factors to consider when choosing an advisor (some additional considerations will be discussed in the next few chapters). A good starting point would be to make sure your advisor is a Certified Financial Planner®. Not only do you then know that the person has a certain level of knowledge in the major disciplines of finance, you also know that he or she must adhere to a Code of Ethics in order to maintain certification.

A CFP® is not necessarily a specialist in a specific area. Some CFP's may also be a CPA or an insurance agent. Good CFPs® will know when it's time to call in a specialist—such as for estate planning or a complicated tax issue. It's important for them to have a good network of people to call on as specific clients' needs arise. By choosing a CFP® you will know that your advisor has a solid base of fundamental knowledge across the disciplines of personal finance.

This may be a good place to explain briefly how Financial Advisors get paid. There are a few basic methods:

- **Commission-based:** the advisor charges a commission each time he or she makes a security trade (buy or sell) for you. The advisor may also earn commissions when selling mutual funds that have sales charges associated with them.
- **Assets under management:** the advisor charges you based on an agreed upon percentage of the assets he or she manages for you. Typically the percentage charged is a sliding scale, declining the more money you've placed under management, or for the type of asset classes managed (varying percentages from equities to fixed income).
- **Hourly-based:** the advisor charges a flat rate per hour.
- A **combination** of some or all of the above.

Finding an advisor that you feel is capable and that you are comfortable working with is a critical first step in managing your money. CFP® or not, if the advisor doesn't relate to you, it's not going to work.

Would You Trust Him with Your Daughter?
Would You Trust Her with Your Son?

"A business that makes nothing but money is a poor kind of business."

-Henry Ford-

Now that Barbara and Mel (remember them from the previous chapter?) had a basic idea of the financial advising profession, they figured it was time to get out there and start meeting some potential candidates.

To get the best sense of their options, they decided they wanted to meet with some people from smaller, boutique-type firms and some people from the large, well known global companies. They came up with a list of people that met their basic criteria and set up the appointments.

Wow, this turned out to be about as much fun as a root canal!

The first person they spoke with didn't seem to be interested in any personal details about Barbara and Mel. It seemed that she had a boilerplate investment plan for everyone in their age bracket. Mel felt that if this was the right strategy, he might as well invest in one of the Life Stage funds and save all the fees of a personal advisor.

The next appointment was with someone that Barbara thought must have sold used cars, or maybe snake oil, in a prior career. He had a fast paced, slick presentation and repeatedly told them about the great returns he could guarantee for them. Barbara and Mel headed home to take a shower.

Mel had his usual weekly golf game the next day and asked around to get some names of advisors to look into. One person's name came up a few times as someone who produced great returns for his clients. When Mel got home that afternoon he called to set up an appointment and got the man's voicemail. No one returned the call, so after a few days, Mel called again. After a week and a half of leaving messages and getting no return call, Mel decided this wasn't the right advisor for them. After all, if he couldn't get the advisor's attention when there was potential new business on the line, what kind of service could he expect to receive once the advisor was sitting on his money? He certainly didn't get a warm and fuzzy feeling about this one.

After taking a break for a few days, Barbara and Mel made their way to an appointment with a smaller firm. The advisor spent a good deal of time trying to get to know them personally. He asked some relevant questions without getting into anything confidential. He then told them about his background, his family, and his philosophy of investing. They were given a tour of the office so that they would be comfortable with the fact that, although the firm was small, it had plenty of support staff to fill their needs.

They didn't sign a contract with him on the spot—they wanted to go home, discuss it privately, and then think on it overnight—they knew as soon as they walked out the door that this was the advisor for them. It took some work and effort to get there, but they were comfortable with their decision.

Professional Perspective

As with any industry, there are some people in financial services who aren't of the highest ethical character. One of your tasks in choosing a financial advisor is to try to weed these people out.

Most financial advisors will meet with you for an hour, at no charge, to find out what you are looking for and to see if you are a good fit for each other. In this initial consultation you should be trying to get a feel for the person. Ask a lot of questions, see how comfortable you feel talking to this person, and pay attention to what your gut is telling you.

I would also recommend that you ask for some references. Don't be shy—after all, you are entrusting your hard-earned money to someone you don't yet know very well.

If the advisor is a CFP®, you can go to the CFP® website and see if any disciplinary action has been taken against him or her. Use this information carefully; in the litigious atmosphere of the country today, the planner may not have done anything wrong but may have been subject to arbitration as opposed to being found guilty.

Remember, in order for advisors to do their jobs, clients must give them the information they need (the subject of the next chapter). If you don't feel comfortable enough with someone to be able to talk to him or her about the personal details of your life, then this person is not the right advisor for you. What you need to look for in an advisor is the expertise to guide you through the process as well as the sensitivity to understand you and your needs.

Smaller firms can be just as secure as larger firms. Your accounts are held at a clearing firm that provides varying levels of insurance against fraud, etc. Choose your advisor and firm based on who can do the best job and offer you the services you need. Larger firms may have more resources at their disposal but may come across as cold and methodical.

It's a Two-Way Street

"Money frees you from doing things you dislike. Since I dislike doing nearly everything, money is handy."

-Groucho Marx-

Barbara and Mel sat around the conference table with their new financial advisor. He explained the details of the letter of engagement to them and they happily signed it. He then pulled out a checklist of documentation he needed them to pull together so he could analyze their situation.

The checklist included: several years of tax returns, several months of mutual fund statements, social security projections, pension plan information from their employers, other retirement savings, and other investments. He also wanted to know about Barbara and Mel's hopes and goals for their children, and any other pertinent information.

They left the advisor's office a little daunted by the task at hand. They were pretty organized, but this was a lot of paper to find and copy.

Mel started to go through their files as soon as they got home. If left to Barbara, he knew, it would never get done, since she was an inveterate procrastinator. The mutual fund statements were easy to locate, as were the other regular investments. Partway through organizing his employee retirement benefits file Mel paused, sat back, and started to think.

He was about to give this man a lot of detailed personal information. Why did the guy need to know about his pension plan? His tax returns contained a lot of personal data—did he really want to be handing it out to people?

Barbara walked into the room and saw the expression on Mel's face. When she asked him what was wrong, he explained that he thought he would give the financial advisor an edited version of the requested information. She was confused—she liked the advisor, and she thought Mel did, too. Mel said he didn't think the advisor needed to see so much material. He was a private person and he'd give the advisor only the information he felt the man needed to know.

Professional Perspective

You can check the credentials of every advisor within a 50-mile radius of your home and I'll bet that you won't find one that lists mind reading or ESP as a skill (that's one set of initials you *won't* see at the end of an advisor's name). There's the old saying, "Garbage in, garbage out." Your advisor can only do a good job for you if he or she is working from good information. If you withhold important information, your advisor will be basing decisions on an incomplete picture of your finances.

Here's an example. Let's say you have a 401(k) through your job. You have your money invested 60% in large cap growth funds, 20% in international funds, and 20% in short term bond funds. You decide that since your advisor won't be handling this money, he doesn't need to know about it. Your advisor develops a plan based upon the assumption that you have no growth stocks in your portfolio. He therefore feels that given your age and risk tolerance you should place 75% of your portfolio in large cap growth stocks. Without knowing it, he has built an out-of-balance portfolio that is weighted too heavily towards large cap growth. You have now subjected yourself to more market volatility and risk than planned on.

Everyone goes to a financial advisor with certain expectations of performance—and rightly so. But you can't expect the advisor to do a good job for you unless you provide the information he or she needs. It may be a pain in the neck to gather the paperwork, or some aspect of your history may be embarrassing, but in the end your advisor will do a better job for you.

To avoid any miscommunication, request an Investment Policy Statement (IPS) that will detail the expectations of both parties, the need for communication, the management or investment philosophy to be employed, as well as the compensation structure. This way neither party can claim to have misunderstood what the objectives were.

Zippidi-Doo-Da

"I'm proud to be paying taxes in the United States. The only thing is—I'd be just as proud for half as much money."

-Arthur Godfrey-

Mel called his new financial advisor on the telephone to explain his concerns about all this information on the checklist. The financial advisor explained to Mel why he needed these things. For example, he needed to see Mel and Barbara's income tax records in order to determine their tax bracket and plan a tax efficient investment strategy. Mel was satisfied with the financial advisor's explanation and proceeded to gather all the records he needed.

Happy with the plan the advisor presented to them at their next meeting, Barbara and Mel confidently transferred their investment and retirement accounts to him. Whew, they were glad this was behind them and someone else was looking out for their financial interests.

The next Saturday night they went out to dinner with another couple with whom they were very friendly. Over dinner they were describing the whole choosing-a-financial-advisor experience. Their friends said that they had been with the same advisor for a number of years but the advisor was now with his fourth firm. Each time the advisor called to say he was moving, they filled out the forms to move their accounts to the new firm with him. They were so confused trying to read the monthly statements from each new firm that by now they weren't really sure what the advisor was doing with their money.

Not only were the new monthly statements bewildering, but the fees and commissions they were paying at this new firm were hard to compare to those at the previous firms.

Mel asked his friend how his returns were at the new firm. His friend said he couldn't tell for sure—some of his investments had to be liquidated in order to move the account, and these had subsequently been reinvested in different places. He didn't understand why this had to be done, but his advisor assured him that he'd get better service and opportunities at this new firm.

Professional Perspective

There are very legitimate reasons for a broker or advisor to move to a different firm. The new firm might offer better advancement opportunities, a corporate culture that is a better fit, or even something as basic as a shorter commute. So don't necessarily assume it's a bad thing if your advisor tells you that he or she is going from Company A to Company B.

On the other hand, some advisors move from company to company to pad their own pocketbook. They might receive signing bonuses based on their bringing a certain number of accounts with them, or there might be other types of incentive packages. For these advisors, a move has nothing to do with providing you with better returns or better service.

Now, there's nothing wrong with an advisor looking to benefit him-or herself financially. That's a primary reason we all work. But, if the advisor has a chronic history of jumping from company to company, you have to question the motivation.

If you get a letter in the mail informing you that your advisor is moving companies, try to determine why. If you have a good relationship, he or she should be able to explain the rationale to you. Before leaving your current company, find out who is handling the accounts left by the departing advisor and meet with that person. Do some research about the new company and see what kind of reputation it has.

Remember, you—and not your financial advisor—are the boss of your money. It is your prerogative to ask questions, and if you don't get that 'warm and cozy' feeling in your gut, you probably should trust your instincts.

Choosing a Financial Advisor—
Quick Recap

- There are many different certifications and specialties in the field of financial planning. When looking for a financial advisor, a good place to start is to make sure your candidates are Certified Financial Planners™. CFPs® are not necessarily specialists, but they have a broad base of financial knowledge and a set of ethical guidelines to uphold.

- Ask a lot of questions when you're meeting with potential advisors. Try to get a feel for how well you can communicate with this person and how much you trust him or her.

- Ask for references.

- Financial advisors need adequate information from you in order to do their jobs. If you withhold financial information from your advisor, the plan he or she develops for you may be heavily skewed towards greater risk or less growth than you'd like.

- If your financial planner switches firms, it might be for perfectly legitimate reasons. On the other hand, he might be putting his needs ahead of yours. Do a little research about the place your advisor is moving to and the reasons for his departure.

- An Investment Policy Statement can help ensure that you and your advisor are on the same page when it comes to your goals, objectives, and expectations.

Conclusion

It's somewhat comforting to know that many of us face the same issues and problems…and make the same mistakes. Although none of us want to admit that we fit a stereotype, most of the stereotypes of financial behavior are based in reality. All of the characters in these stories are modeled on real people facing real circumstances. They have been over-dramatized only to add some humor and emphasize a point.

If the title of this book is correct, then maybe money problems are a little funnier when it's someone else's money. But to the extent that we recognize ourselves in these characters, we're also poking fun at ourselves, and there's nothing wrong with that! Hopefully you've enjoyed reading about these bizarre and quirky people. Equally as important, I hope I've been able to present some useful information in a fun way.

It's Not So Funny When It's Your Money is not intended to be a personal finance textbook and shouldn't be used as the ultimate reference for your financial planning needs and solutions. If it has made you a little more knowledgeable about the issues you should be aware of, the book has been successful.

Whether you're a do-it-yourselfer or happy to completely delegate to advisors, managing your financial affairs effectively will play a key role in successfully achieving a balanced life—however you personally define that balance.

NOTES AND DISCLOSURES

[1] Contribution limits vary by state. Contributions to a Section 529 plan are subject to applicable limits under federal gift tax and generation skipping transfer tax provisions and may be subject, upon distribution, to federal income tax if the amounts are not used for higher educational expenses. Penalties, in accordance with IRS guidelines, may apply to distributions that are not attributable to higher educational expenses of the designated beneficiary, made on account of the death or disability of the beneficiary, or due to rollover. Withdrawals for non-qualified educational expenses are subject to a 10% federal tax penalty and are taxed as ordinary income.

State tax advantages vary from state to state and may depend on whether you are a resident of the state sponsoring the plan. As with other investments, there are generally fees and expenses associated with participation in Section 529 College Savings Plans. Fees and expenses vary greatly, even among plans offered within the same state. There is also the risk that plan investments may lose money or not perform well enough to cover college costs as anticipated.

[2] The Morningstar name and trademarks are used under license from Morningstar Associates, LLC. Investment advisory products and services are provided by Morningstar Associates, LLC, a registered investment advisor and a wholly owned subsidiary of Morningstar, Inc. Morningstar Associates, LLC is not an affiliate of NFP Securities, Inc.

Securities and Advisory Services offered through NFP Securities, Inc.
A Broker/Dealer, Member NASD, SIPC and Federally Registered Investment Advisor
NFP Securities, Inc. is not affiliated with ASAM

This book is for informational purposes only. Neither Andrew Stuart Asset Management nor NFP Securities, Inc. offers legal advice. Please consult with an attorney regarding your specific circumstances.

While all the case information is accurate, it has been altered to protect client identity. The investment strategies discussed are for illustrative purposes only and should not be deemed a representation or guarantee of past or future results. These examples do not represent any specific product.

Using diversification allocation as part of your investment strategy neither assures nor guarantees better performance and cannot protect against loss in declining markets.

IRS Circular 230 disclosure:

INDEX

978-0-595-40916-7
0-595-40916-4